BY THE EDITORS OF
CONSUMER GUIDE®

A BEGINNER'S GUIDE TO A COLORFUL GARDEN

Contributing Authors:
Carol Landa Christensen
Ted Marston

Consultants:
Judy Glattstein
Dr. Steven Still

Illustrator:
Mike Muir

Louis Weber, C.E.O.
Publications International, Ltd.
7373 North Cicero Avenue
Lincolnwood, IL 60646

Manufactured in the USA.

8 7 6 5 4 3 2 1

ISBN 1-56173-753-4

Contributing Authors:

Carol Landa Christensen graduated *cum laude* from the Pennsylvania School of Horticulture for Women, and went on to work at Longwood Gardens as a Horticultural Information Specialist and as a floral designer. She has written flower gardening features regularly for newspapers and *Gurney's Gardening News.*

Ted Marston has been writing about gardens and gardening for 20 years. His articles have appeared in national publications such as *The New York Times, Family Circle,* and *Flower and Garden,* and he has edited several gardening periodicals and books, including *Plants Alive.*

Consultants:

Judy Glattstein has been a landscape consultant since 1976. She is a frequent contributor to national horticultural publications such as *Horticulture, Garden Designs, Flower and Garden,* and the Brooklyn Botanic Garden Handbook, *Plants for Problem Places.* Ms. Glattstein is also a workshop instructor and lecturer.

Dr. Steven Still is a Professor of Horticulture at The Ohio State University and author of the widely used textbook, *Manual of Herbaceous Ornamental Plants.* Photographs from Dr. Still's extensive picture library appear frequently in many horticultural publications.

Photo Credits:

Front and back cover photos: Steven M. Still

FPG: Dennis Hallinan: 24; **Photo/Nats:** Liz Ball: 26; Gay Bumgarner: 12, 28, 32 (top), 35; Don Johnston: 20; John Lynch: 52 (right), 54 (center); Ann Reilly: 14, 22, 48 (left), 53 (left); **Rainbow:** Coco McCoy: 59 (left); Dan McCoy: 52 (left); **Steven M. Still:** 3, 4, 5, 6, 8, 18, 30, 38, 42, 43, 44, 45, 46, 47, 48, 49, 50, 51, 52, 53, 54, 55, 56, 57, 58, 59, 60, 61, 62, 63, 64.

CONTENTS

This beautifully planned garden of sweet alyssum, floss flowers, and petunias is visual proof of the beauty of annuals.

Introduction

Annuals come in all shapes, sizes, and colors.

Annuals are those plants that go through an entire life cycle—germinate, grow, flower, produce seed, and die—all in a single growing season. Generally, they reach the point of flower production within six to eight weeks after sprouting and continue in abundant bloom until they're killed by frost. No wonder, then, that annuals are such a boon to gardeners! Most grow quickly and easily, provide a long season of color, and require minimal special care at very low cost. They also offer a wondrous variety of sizes, flower forms, and leaf types from which to choose. A gardener's problem is not whether to grow annuals—it's how to narrow the choice to those few that space allows.

Since annuals are so easy to grow, sooner or later most of us will decide to try our hand at growing a few favorites. This book will tell you how to take full advantage of annuals gardening. You will first learn how to prepare your soil and use the available light to best advantage. Then you will be taken through the various methods of annuals planting—bedding plants, sowing seeds, and propagating stem cuttings—so that you can make the best choice for your garden.

Also included are tips that will help make your summer's work much easier: how to weed and water, as well as explanations of feeding and plant staking alternatives. An illustrated section that allows easy identification of garden pests and diseases contains recommendations for dealing with each problem. The directory features descriptions, how-to-grow techniques, propagation, uses, and related species and varieties for at-a-glance information about the most common annuals.

Whether you have a large yard, a small one, or just a balcony, you'll find ideas here for ways to appreciate the beauty of annuals and enjoy the experience of planning your own garden. As you become more comfortable with annuals gardening, you'll find yourself gradually increasing both the amount and the varieties you plant!

Planning a Seasonal Kaleidoscope of Color

Proper soil and light are the keys to gardening success.

Soil and Light

Soil and light are especially important factors to consider when planning an annuals garden. Soil types vary from the extremes of constantly dry, nutrient-poor sand to 90 percent rocks held together with 10 percent soil to rich, heavy clay (which forms a slick, sticky, shoe-grabbing mass when wet, then dries to brick hardness). Fortunately, most soil conditions fall somewhere between these extremes. Still, very few homeowners find they have that ideal "rich garden loam" to work with!

Therefore, the first order of business is to learn just what kind of soil you *do* have. The way to do this is to have your soil tested. In some states, the county Cooperative Extension office will do soil tests; in others, it's necessary to use the services of a private testing lab.

To obtain a representative sample of the soil in your flower bed, take a tablespoonful from each end of the bed and another from somewhere in the middle. Dig 4 to 6 inches down before taking each sample. Mix all of the samples together thoroughly in a single container. Then hand carry or mail the mixture to those doing the testing.

You'll want a complete soil test. One part will be a pH test that reads for acidity or alkalinity. A pH test result between 6.0 and 7.0 is ideal and requires no adjustment. A result below 6.0 indicates the soil is too acidic. Ground limestone should be added to correct this problem. If the reading is over 7.2, the soil is too alkaline. To alleviate this condition, add powdered sulphur or, for quicker results, iron sulfate.

In addition to pH, you'll receive information about the nutrients in your soil. If there is a deficiency in any of these, you'll need to add the missing elements as recommended in the report. A third result will tell you the percentage of organic materials contained in your soil; this information will help you decide whether or not you need to supplement your soil with additional organic matter. (Further details on fertilizing and improving garden soil can be found in "Preparing the Soil," page 12.)

Some homesites have so little soil or the soil is so poor that it cannot—or should not—be used at all. One solution in these situations is to build raised beds and fill them with high-quality soil brought in from elsewhere. Such beds should be at least 6 inches deep to allow good root penetration. This may seem a costly solution in the short term, but the beds will last for years and prove themselves well worth your initial investment.

Another solution, especially in a small area, is to garden entirely in containers. An imaginative approach, such as installing a deck or patio over the useless ground and then decorating it with container-grown plants, can turn an eyesore into an oasis. (You'll find more details on container gardening on page 38.)

Light is another important factor in gardening. How much is there and for how many hours each day? In other words, does the area where you want to grow your flowers have full sun, partial shade, or full shade? At least to some extent, the amount of light the flower bed receives will dictate the plant species you'll be able to grow. Those plants that love full sun may become leggy and produce very few flowers if they're planted in a shady spot. By the same token, some plants are sensitive to too much light and will burn when placed in bright sunlight. Fortunately, there are annuals for all lighting conditions. Therefore, except for those places of deepest shade, there are many different annuals from which to choose.

Testing for Soil Type

Soil may vary from light sand to heavy clay. A rough test can be made by squeezing a wettened sample in your hand. If it falls apart easily, it's primarily sand; if it forms a solid, sticky glob, it's primarily clay. The ideal growing medium is somewhere between the two; by adding conditioners and humus to your soil, you can make it closer to that ideal. Send a soil sample to a testing lab to learn what additives and nutrients your soil needs.

Obtaining a Soil Sample

To obtain a good representative sample of garden soil for testing, dig down 3 to 6 inches below the surface in several different locations in the planting bed. Take a tablespoonful from each hole. Mix all of the samples together thoroughly to make one single large sample. Then hand carry or mail this single sample to the testing lab for analysis. Soil samples can be taken in the fall if you want to add slow-acting pH adjusters during the fall or winter months.

Gardening with Raised Beds

Raised beds are a good choice where soil is either of particularly poor quality or non-existent. Constructed of pressure-treated wood, reinforced concrete, or mortared brick, stone, or blocks, these beds can be of any length, but should have a soil depth of at least 6 inches. For easy maintenance, beds should be no wider than 4 feet. By filling some beds with a rich loam mixture and others with a more sandy, well-drained mix, it's possible to provide the ideal soil requirements for a wide range of plants.

Attractive Annuals Choices

Annual plantings will have more impact if, as part of the planning process, you consider *all* that each variety has to offer. Frequently, we only think about the color of the flowers annuals produce: Will pale pink petunias look best beside blue asters, or would bright pink be better?

Color is an important factor, but many plants have even more to offer. They may have both colorful blooms *and* foliage of an unusual texture or color: bold-leaved geraniums and nasturtiums; purple-red cockscomb leaves; and feathery baby's breath. Or they may be grown primarily, or even exclusively, for their foliage. Outstanding examples are silvery gray dusty miller and the myriad colors of coleus. Texture, or surface, can also be intriguing. Think of airy baby's breath in contrast to bold and massive marigolds. Form of both flowers and of the overall habit should also be considered. Flower forms include tall spikes, round globes, sprays, and clusters. Plant forms range from tall and skinny to low and spreading.

In addition, scale (the size of a plant) must also be kept in mind. Miniature plants are great to use in small spaces and where people are close enough to see them, but in a large area, they can become completely lost. On the other hand, large-growing plants such as nasturtiums may dominate and even smother out smaller neighbors when space is limited.

When selecting plants to be combined in a garden, all of these factors should be taken into consideration at the time of planning. The design will be more effective if a pleasing mixture of contrasting textures, colors, and plant and flower forms is used.

The easiest, most straightforward way to use annuals is to select one favorite and flood the entire planting area with it. This approach eliminates deciding where to plant a particular variety, selecting colors and textures that blend together effectively, or learning the cultural requirements for more than one kind of plant. It can be a money-saving solution as well: You only need to purchase one or two seed packets to obtain enough plants to fill an entire planting area. Another way to mass annuals is to keep to a single color but use several different plant varieties. The resulting garden would contain plants of different forms and heights with a variety of different flower shapes, all in varying shades of one color.

What a pleasing mixture of contrasting textures, colors, and forms!

Although annuals make a splendid display on their own, they also combine effectively with other plants. Consider adding several strategically located accent clumps in shrub plantings. Annuals can also provide the perfect mid-summer boost to a perennials border—whether in an area where spring bulbs are dying back or where early flowering biennials have been removed. Another good place to add annuals is in the vegetable patch. Not only will they enliven an area not normally expected to be colorful, they will also provide an excellent source of cut flowers to bring indoors.

The charts that follow are a quick reference for selecting plants for your garden. However, it should be kept in mind that they give only a simplistic first screening. When scanning these lists, you may find many plants that seem appropriate for your garden. However, on further investigation, you'll find that some of them aren't appropriate at all. Use the charts to narrow down the choices; then refer to the more detailed description in the directory section, beginning on page 42, to identify those well-suited to your climate, soil, and light conditions.

These charts are very easy to use, since they identify plants by color range (in most cases by flower color). However, those marked with an asterisk (*) have colorful foliage, fruits, or seedpods instead.

It is important to remember that the "multicolor" category lists those plants that come in nearly every color range (any annual that comes in more than three color ranges has been put into this category). Because it contains the most universal and versatile annuals, be sure to use it often when making your selections.

Whether you are a novice or a gardener with many years of planting experience, using a chart with information on color, light, soil, and height can make the difference between a picture-perfect garden and one that just doesn't quite work.

The Varied Characteristics of Annuals

Flowers are not the sole source of color in annual gardens. Many plants, such as this muted dusty miller and more dramatic purple perilla, are treasured for their foliage alone. Others, such as cockscombs, have both colorful foliage *and* flowers.

The broad, velvety leaves of this flowering tobacco, as well as its tall spikes of trumpet-shaped flowers, are a complete contrast in form to the low-spreading impatiens. A garden is more visually stimulating when a variety of forms is used.

Variety of scale can be provided by both flowers and plants. Here, a large, wide-spreading cosmos and compact calliopsis provide similar flowers on very different-sized plants. Other species, zinnias, for example, offer a wide range of flower sizes and forms on plants that are all very much alike in form and size. Make use of this full range of flower and plant size to provide interest in your garden.

This cloud of baby's breath illustrates the role that texture can play in a garden. A flower bed planted exclusively with such open, airy plants would appear to be a floating mist. By contrast, a bed planted entirely with bold, massive plants such as these marigolds would be heavy and solid-looking. Mixing plants of differing textures provides a pleasant variety and balance.

Selecting Annuals for Color and Characteristics

	Dry Soil	Average Soil	Moist Soil	Full Sun	Part Shade	Full Shade	Under 12 Inches	12-24 Inches	Over 24 Inches	Vining
MULTICOLOR										
Amaranth, Globe	•	•		•				•		
Begonia, Fibrous		•		•	•	•	•			
Begonia, Tuberous*		•	•		•	•		•		
Coleus*			•		•	•		•		
Cosmos		•		•				•	•	
Dahlia		•	•	•				•	•	
Daisy, Transvaal		•	•	•			•	•		
Everlastings	•	•		•				•		
Gazania	•			•			•	•		
Geranium, Ivy-Leaf		•		•	•		•	•	•	
Geranium, Other			•	•				•		
Geranium, Zonal			•	•				•		
Hollyhock		•	•	•					•	
Impatiens		•	•		•	•	•	•		
Impatiens, New Guinea		•	•	•				•		
Nicotiana		•	•	•	•			•	•	
Pansy		•	•	•	•		•			
Petunia		•		•				•		
Phlox		•		•			•	•		
Portulaca	•			•			•			
Primrose		•	•		•		•			
Snapdragon		•		•			•	•	•	
Verbena	•	•		•			•			
Zinnia		•		•			•	•	•	

	Dry Soil	Average Soil	Moist Soil	Full Sun	Part Shade	Full Shade	Under 12 Inches	12-24 Inches	Over 24 Inches	Vining
BLUE TO PURPLE										
Alyssum, Sweet	•	•		•			•			
Aster		•		•			•	•	•	
Bachelor's Button		•	•	•				•	•	
Floss Flower		•		•	•		•			
Forget-Me-Not		•	•	•	•		•			
Fuchsia		•	•		•			•		
Larkspur		•		•				•	•	
Lisianthus		•	•	•				•	•	
Lobelia		•	•	•	•		•			
Salvia		•		•	•		•	•	•	
Stock		•	•	•				•	•	
RED										
Blanket Flower	•			•				•		
China Pink	•	•		•			•			
Cockscomb		•		•			•	•	•	
Hibiscus, Chinese			•	•					•	
Marigold, Pot		•		•			•	•		
Monkey Flower			•		•		•			
Nasturtium	•	•		•			•			•
Salvia		•		•	•		•	•	•	
Stock		•		•				•	•	
Vinca		•	•	•			•	•		

*= foliage or fruits/pods this color

PINK TO FUCHSIA	Dry Soil	Average Soil	Moist Soil	Full Sun	Part Shade	Full Shade	Under 12 Inches	12-24 Inches	Over 24 Inches	Vining
Alyssum, Sweet	•	•		•			•			
Aster		•		•			•	•	•	
Baby's Breath		•		•				•		
Bachelor's Button		•	•	•				•	•	
China Pink	•	•		•			•			
Cleome		•		•					•	
Cockscomb		•		•			•	•	•	
Forget-Me-Not		•	•	•	•		•			
Fuchsia		•	•		•			•		
Hibiscus, Chinese			•	•					•	
Larkspur		•		•				•	•	
Lisianthus		•	•	•				•	•	
Lobelia		•	•	•	•		•			
Monkey Flower			•		•		•			
Ornamental Cabbage, Kale		•		•				•		
Stock		•	•	•				•	•	
Vinca		•	•	•			•	•		

YELLOW TO ORANGE	Dry Soil	Average Soil	Moist Soil	Full Sun	Part Shade	Full Shade	Under 12 Inches	12-24 Inches	Over 24 Inches	Vining
Black-Eyed Susan	•	•		•				•	•	
Blanket Flower	•			•				•		
Cockscomb		•		•			•	•	•	
Hibiscus, Chinese			•	•					•	
Marigold, American			•	•				•	•	
Marigold, French			•	•			•			
Marigold, Pot		•		•			•	•		
Meadow Foam			•	•			•			
Monkey Flower			•		•		•			
Nasturtium	•	•		•			•			•
Sanvitalia	•	•		•	•		•			
Sunflower		•		•					•	

GRASSES & FOLIAGE	Dry Soil	Average Soil	Moist Soil	Full Sun	Part Shade	Full Shade	Under 12 Inches	12-24 Inches	Over 24 Inches	Vining
Amaranth, Globe	•	•		•					•	
Begonia, Tuberous		•	•		•	•		•		
Coleus		•	•		•	•		•		
Dusty Miller	•	•		•			•	•		
Geranium, Ivy-Leaf		•		•	•				•	
Geranium, Other			•	•				•		
Geranium, Zonal			•	•				•		
Impatiens, New Guinea		•	•	•				•		
Ornamental Cabbage, Kale		•		•				•		

WHITE TO GREEN	Dry Soil	Average Soil	Moist Soil	Full Sun	Part Shade	Full Shade	Under 12 Inches	12-24 Inches	Over 24 Inches	Vining
Alyssum, Sweet	•	•		•			•			
Aster		•		•			•	•	•	
Baby's Breath		•		•				•		
Bachelor's Button		•	•	•				•	•	
China Pink	•	•		•			•			
Cleome		•		•					•	
Floss Flower		•		•	•		•			
Forget-Me-Not		•	•	•	•		•			
Hibiscus, Chinese			•	•					•	
Larkspur		•		•				•	•	
Lisianthus		•	•	•				•	•	
Lobelia		•	•	•	•		•			
Marigold, American			•	•				•	•	
Marigold, Pot		•		•			•	•		
Ornamental Cabbage, Kale*		•		•				•		
Salvia		•		•	•		•	•	•	
Stock		•	•	•				•	•	
Vinca		•	•	•			•	•		

These cultural recommendations are intended to suggest the average conditions over a widespread geographical area. It is important to be aware of local requirements.

Secrets to Sucessful Annuals Gardening

Preparing the Soil

As was mentioned in the section on soil and light on page 6, soil characteristics vary widely. Naturally, then, there's also wide variation in the ways to amend and improve soil to achieve the best possible growing conditions.

If the results of your soil test indicate a lack of certain nutrients, you should follow the recommendations made by the testing company for supplementing the soil. If the imbalance is slight, organic fertilizers can be used. Because they generally contain a low percentage of nutrients that are slowly released into the soil, organic fertilizers are inadequate when fast results are needed, or if the imbalance of nutrients is great. In these situations, inorganic fertilizers are the better choice. A combination of both kinds may be a good compromise solution, using the quick-to-feed commercial plant foods first, then following up in subsequent years with the slow-feeding organic fertilizers.

Chemical fertilizer is commonly formulated in some combination of the three major nutrients: nitrogen, phosphorous, and potassium—N, P, K. The numbers featured on each bag represent the percentage of each of these nutrients in the mix. For example, 5-10-5 contains 5 percent nitrogen (N), 10 percent phosphorous (P), and 5 percent potassium (K). 10-10-10 contains 10 percent of each. The NPK formula is also listed on each container of organic fertilizer. The percentages of each nutrient are lower in organic fertilizers than in inorganic fertilizers. Therefore, larger amounts of organic plant food are required to achieve the same results.

It's also possible to purchase fertilizers separately rather than in a three-nutrient mix. These are useful when there's a deficiency in a single nutrient. Consult with your Cooperative Extension office (there's one in every county) or garden center staff if you feel uncertain about solving nutrient deficiency problems.

Well-prepared soil helps plants grow better.

Adjusting the nutrient and pH levels in your soil will not make any difference in its *consistency*. Improving soil texture will require the addition of one or several "soil conditioners." The most commonly used conditioners are leaf mold, compost, well-rotted cow manure, and peat moss. Vermiculite, perlite, and sand (coarse builder's sand; *never* use beach sand) can also be added, especially when the basic soil is heavy.

To properly prepare a planting bed, first remove any sod from the area, then rototill or hand dig the soil, turning it over thoroughly. (Rototillers can be rented by the day, and it's often possible to hire someone to come and till by the hour, if you don't have a tiller of your own.)

If the area is rocky, remove as many stones as possible as you till. Next, spread the necessary fertilizer, soil conditioners, and pH-adjusting chemicals over the area. Till again. You should be able to till more deeply the second time; ideally, you want to loosen and improve the soil to a depth of more than 6 inches. Turn and loosen soil by hand with a spade where the area is too small to require a Rototiller. After this initial treatment, fertilizers, soil conditioners, and pH-adjusting chemicals will be added at different times of the year for best results.

If possible, allow the soil to stand unplanted for a week or more. Stir the surface inch or two every three to four days with a scuffle hoe or cultivator to eradicate fast-germinating weed seeds. This will make your weeding chores lighter during the rest of the season.

Now is the perfect time to install some kind of mowing strip around the garden bed. Patio squares or slate pieces laid end-to-end at ground level will keep grass and flowers from intermixing. Other options include landscape logs, poured concrete strips, or bricks laid side-by-side on a sand or concrete base. The mowing strip must be deep and wide enough so grass roots cannot tunnel underneath or travel across the top to reach the flower bed, and the top of the strip must not extend above the level of the adjacent lawn.

Over time, a mowing strip will save more gardening effort, to say nothing of the gardener's patience, than any other device. It's well worth the time and money invested at the beginning!

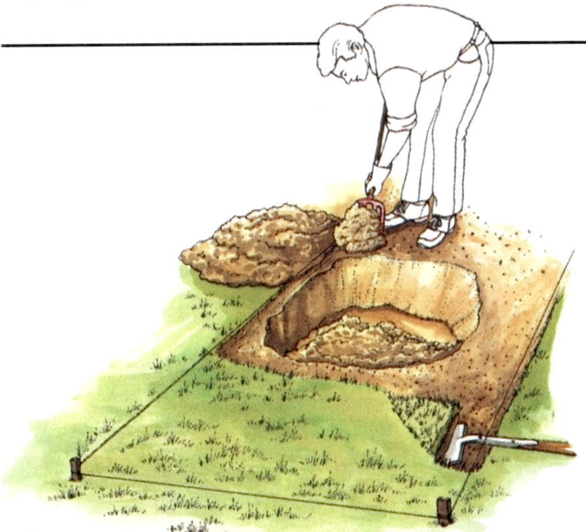

Planting Preparations

1 Mark the flower bed boundaries with pegs and string for straight edges and with a garden hose for curved lines. Cut through the sod along laid-out lines with a spade. Remove the sod from the entire bed. Till the area, removing rocks as you proceed. For a small planting area, dig and break up the soil by hand or with a spade.

2 Spread well-rotted manure, compost, or leaf mold onto the bed to provide organic matter and improve soil quality. If other soil conditioners are needed, perlite, sand, and moistened peat moss should be added at this time.

3 Rototill or hand dig the bed deeply a second time to thoroughly incorporate these additions. This second digging will allow the tiller to loosen soil to a greater depth than could be achieved by tilling only once.

4 To keep the grass out of the flower bed and the annuals from overflowing onto the lawn, install an edging strip around the bed. This strip should be at least 2 inches deep and 6 inches wide. The top of the strip should be at ground level to allow the wheel of the lawnmower to run along it. Installation of an edging strip will save many hours of maintenance effort each year.

Bedding Plants by the Boxful

For those who want to have an almost instant show of annual bloom, boxed bedding plants are the answer. Every garden center and nursery, many roadside stands, and quite a few grocery and discount stores offer a selection of prestarted annuals. These plants are timed to be at the blooming stage on the normal date of the last spring frost. Thus, they can be planted as soon as they're purchased. Most will provide floral color in two weeks or less, after which they'll continue to supply bloom steadily until autumn's first freeze.

The main drawback to purchasing boxed bedding plants is the limited selection. Nearly all suppliers offer several varieties each of marigolds, geraniums, asters, zinnias, petunias, and impatiens. Some will carry a few additional species such as coleus, snapdragons, and salvia. But there are so many lovely annuals that are less well-known, and therefore unavailable from any commercial sources. A gardener who wants them will have to start them at home. Also, if large numbers of plants are needed, the cost of purchasing them as boxed plants can become prohibitive for those with limited funds.

PLANTS TO START INDOORS

Globe Amaranth	Impatiens
Aster	Lisianthus
Fibrous Begonia	Lobelia
Tuberous Begonia	Nicotiana
Cleome	Pansy
Coleus	Petunia
Dahlia	Salvia
African Daisy	Snapdragon
Dusty Miller	Stock
Floss Flower	Verbena
Geranium	Vinca

(Note: Some plants will be found on both this list and the list of plants to sow directly in the garden. Either option will work; you may want to start those with short growing seasons indoors in order to enjoy the longest possible period of bloom.)

Buying boxed bedding plants is very popular.

In these instances, or just for the pleasure of it, you may want to start your own bedding plants. It's quite possible for any gardener to succeed with only a small initial investment in equipment and supplies.

LIGHT—The most essential ingredient for successful seed starting is adequate light. It's possible to start seeds on the sill of a sun-filled window, but plants often stretch out toward the light source and become leggy. A three-sided white or silver reflector shield set up behind the plant trays will reflect light back onto the plants to help combat this problem.

Where there is not enough light available naturally, an easy and not very expensive alternative is to raise seedlings under fluorescent growlamps. Garden catalogs feature ready-made light units, or you can easily design your own. Turned on and off by a timer, such a setup can be located anywhere in the house, even in a storage area that is normally unlit. To provide maximum light from all sides, surround the area under the lights with a white or silver-painted reflector. This will bounce light back onto the plants, and result in well-rounded, compact bedding plants.

HEAT—Along with light, another important need is adequate heat. Interestingly, the surrounding air temperature is not nearly so important as bottom heat that warms the soil in which the seedlings are grown. A furnace room or any other regularly heated area will provide a good growing environment. If the air temperature in the chosen growing area is colder than 70° F, bottom heat can be supplied by a heating

1

Equipment and Supplies for Starting Plants Indoors

The equipment needed for starting plants indoors includes:

* A fluorescent light fixture with full-spectrum growlamp bulbs. Ideally, you should be able to easily raise and lower the fixture in order to maintain about 3 inches between the light bulbs and the plant tops at all times.

* An automatic timer to turn the light fixture on and off each day is optional. However, it does take the worry out of trying to remember this twice-a-day chore. Since plants require between 16 to 18 hours of light daily, don't leave the lights on all of the time; darkness is also essential.

* White or silver-colored reflectors placed around three, or all four, sides will bounce light onto plants from all angles. It will help keep them from leaning and stretching toward a single light source. A home-made reflector can be made of cardboard covered with aluminum foil.

* If the seed starting setup is in a cool room, a thermostatically controlled heating cable should be laid under the seed boxes and pots. Bottom heat is more important than air temperature to encourage strong growth.

* A drip tray allows watering of seedlings from the bottom. Water poured into the tray is absorbed upward into the soil.

cable installed under the growing medium. Safe, thermostatically controlled cables designed for this use can be obtained from most garden suppliers.

WATER—After light and heat, water is a third requirement for plant growth. A rimmed watering tray will allow the seed trays and young plants to be watered from the bottom. Top watering can batter plants down, as well as increase the possibility of fungus problems.

The primary concern with bottom watering is overwatering. Water shouldn't continuously stand in the watering tray. If it does, the plant roots will drown for lack of oxygen. The way to avoid this problem, and still be sure of giving *enough* water, is to pour water to a ¼-inch depth into the tray. Leave it for five to ten minutes—this will give the water time to be pulled up into the planting soil. At the end of that time, observe how much water, if any, is left in the tray. Also, roll a small pinch of the planting soil between thumb and finger to test for moisture. If the soil feels dry and all of the water in the tray is gone, pour some more water in and go through the waiting and testing process again. What you want is soil that feels wet with very little or no water remaining in the tray. If the soil is wet and the tray is full of water, remove

2 Sowing Seeds

For a small number of seeds, plant two seeds per starting cube, then remove the weaker seedling when they grow their second, true leaves. Or plant seeds in rows—one or two rows per variety—in a seed tray. For larger quantities, sprinkle a packet of seeds over the entire seed tray. *Be sure to label* each row or tray; otherwise, seedlings can be difficult to identify by sight.

the excess water from the tray with a turkey baster. Don't worry about the last ⅛ inch of water; it will evaporate away in a day or less, which is not long enough to cause a problem.

Test the soil moisture once each day by rolling a small amount between your fingers. Water again when the soil feels more dry than wet, but don't wait for it to become bone dry. It's impossible to predict how many days will be needed between waterings as so many factors come into play: the humidity of the room, whether the days were sunny or overcast, how large the plants are, and the makeup of the soil mix. You'll be able to make a fairly accurate "guesstimate" of your own circumstances after a few weeks, but it's still a good idea to do a pinch test each day just to double-check.

SOIL—Planting soil for starting and growing young seedlings should be free of weeds and disease. This can be accomplished by sterilizing the planting mix. First, spread it in a thin layer on cookie sheets and bake at a low temperature (150 to 200° F) until it stops steaming and is completely dried out. Next, cool the soil and mix the water back into it until it's moist but not muddy. Finally, pour the soil into sterile containers, allowing it to settle for a day before planting the seeds. A far simpler approach is to purchase a specially formulated plant starter mix made up of inert materials. Fill the sterile containers with this mix, firm or tamp it lightly with your fingers, then sow the seeds.

CONTAINERS—Seeds can be started in a variety of containers: milk or egg cartons with holes punched in their bottoms or low on their sides, plastic or wooden boxes, clay or plastic pots, peat pots, or special seed starter cubes and trays are all equally acceptable. Virtually anything that will hold soil and allow easy passage of water through drainage holes in the bottom will work.

Containers designed to hold a single plant are the best choice for large plants, which tend to crowd each other out in six-packs, and for plants that don't like to have their roots disturbed by transplanting. Most annuals do well in any container, making the choice a matter of personal preference.

SOWING SEEDS—Seeds can be sown individually in single pots. Plant two seeds in each, removing the weaker of the two seedlings when they grow their first real leaves (the very first leaves to unfold from a new seedling are called the seed leaves; the second set of leaves is its first real leaves).

When sowing a packet of seeds in a box or larger pot, they can either be broadcast over the surface in a scatter pattern or be planted in rows. If only a few plants of each kind are wanted, rows make more sense; when larger numbers of plants are desired, broadcasting is faster. If the seeds are very small, don't cover them with additional planting mix after sowing; medium to large seeds (those larger than sugar granules) should have a layer of planting mix sprinkled on top. A rule of thumb is to cover them to a depth equal to their thickness. Lightly press the surface of the planting mix after sowing to settle the soil particles firmly around the seeds.

LABEL—*Be sure to label* each planting in some way. You think you'll be able to remember where you planted each kind of seed, but most of the time you won't! Either write the name on wooden or plastic labels and insert them in the soil at the end of each row or slide the empty seed packet along the container edge with the name showing. You can even color code or otherwise mark each container, making a list of the varieties that match each code mark.

Once the seeds are sown, water the seed trays from the bottom until the mix feels moist when you lightly press a finger on its surface. Allow excess water to drip out of the container bottom (remember, whatever type container you use, it must have drainage holes in the bottom to allow water flow) before placing the container in the growing setup you've prepared.

Lay two sheets of newspaper over each seed tray. For the first few days, this provides the semi-darkness some seeds prefer for germination. Inspect each seed tray closely every day. As soon as you see seedlings pushing through, remove the newspaper layer. Germination time varies widely. Don't worry if some varieties haven't yet sprouted while others planted at the same time have already grown an inch or more. Ideally, though, you should start the slower growers earlier than those that germinate rapidly in order to have them all at the same stage when planting time arrives. Study the descriptions of each plant to know when to get each of them started.

DAMPING OFF—Probably the worst enemy of successful seed starting is a problem known as "damping off." It strikes within two weeks of germination when seedlings are very young. When it hits, the plants simply lie down and die, usually in less than a day's time. Damping off is a fungus infection that can best be avoided by making certain that both the soil and containers in which seeds are planted are sterile. The seeds themselves can be lightly dusted with fungicide powder prior to planting as an additional precaution. However, sometimes even with the best efforts, contamination still takes place. Therefore, young seedlings should be looked at morning and evening to check for any sign of a problem. Even if only two or three plants have lain down, take the

3 Transplanting Seedlings

Except when planted in individual cubes, seedlings should be transplanted from seed starter trays when they grow their first set of true leaves. Hold a seed leaf (*never* hold by the stem at this stage) and lift the soil from underneath it with a fork or similar tool, gently removing the seedling. Insert it in a hole already poked in the soil of a six-pack or peat pot. The soil level on the plant stem should be the same in the new planter as it was in the seed tray. Firm the soil around the roots with your fingers. Water to firm the soil more. Plants remain in these containers until they're planted outdoors or into planters for the summer.

These newly planted begonias have a lot of growing to do.

precaution of immediately spraying the plants with a fungicide or, if none is available, try a mild vinegar solution (one part vinegar to four parts water).

FOOD—Prepared starter mixes usually have plant nutrients in them that slowly release to feed the seedlings. If you make your own homemade starter from milled sphagnum, vermiculite, or sterilized sand, you'll need to fertilize in some way. The easiest method is to add a soluble fertilizer at a very weak rate to the regular waterings. (For details on various organic and inorganic fertilizers, read "Feeding Alternatives," page 28.)

PRICKING OFF—Other than those that were planted individually, all seedlings should be transplanted from the seed trays when the first true leaves appear. This first transplanting is usually referred to as "pricking off." At this stage, seedlings should be planted into small individual peat pots, planting cubes, or partitioned growing boxes. They will remain in these containers until it's time for them to be planted in the garden.

Fill the boxes with a good potting soil or commercial growing mix. To make your own soil, mix together equal amounts of garden soil or sterilized potting soil, moistened peat moss, and perlite or coarse builder's sand. Gently lift out and separate the young plants, holding them by their seed leaves. Never hold them by the stem—stems can easily be permanently injured by too much heat or pressure, thereby killing the plant. However, if a seed leaf is broken off, the plant will easily survive and thrive if it is taken care of properly.

Place the seedling in the new container so the soil line will be at the same level on the stem as it was in the seed tray. Gently firm the soil around the plant roots, then add more soil, if necessary, to bring it to within ¼ inch of the container rim. Water from the top with a weak fertilizer solution to further firm the soil around the plant and get it off to a good start. Place these pricked-off plants back by the window or under growlamps to continue their growth until a couple of weeks before you plan to plant them outdoors.

HARDENING OFF—By this time, plants should be stocky and strong, but they will need some toughening up before their succulent foliage will be able to survive outdoor conditions. This process is referred to as "hardening off," and is very important for a smooth transition from indoors to outside. It'll keep the plants from suffering shock, which at best will detain their growth for a couple of weeks.

The process isn't difficult. Simply carry the plants outdoors each day for a few hours, bringing them back inside overnight. Always shade them with an old window screen to protect them from strong light and wind. Start with two or three hours, then increase the length of time they're outside by an additional hour each day. After a week, they can be outdoors all day, and only need to be brought in at night to avoid possible danger of frost.

PLANTING OUT—At this point, the plants are ready to plant out into the prepared garden bed. Those in individual peat pots can be dropped right into planting holes, the soil firmed around the pot, an earth dam formed around the stem to form a water-holding area, and a weak fertilizer solution poured in to fill the bowl thus formed. This watering will help settle the soil and eliminate air pockets around the root-ball.

Plants in multi-plant containers will need to be turned out of the container and separated before planting. Water the plants well before attempting to remove them. If the soil is moist, they'll slide out easily, subjecting the plants to less shock. Some roots are bound to be broken off in this process; pinching out the top growth on the plant will help keep the top and root areas in balance. This pinching will also encourage side shoots to push out, helping to form a fuller flowering plant.

Replant quickly so the tender roots don't dry out in the wind or sun. Follow the same procedures for planting and watering as for transplanting into peat pots for healthy and vigorous plant growth.

SHADING—If possible, do your transplanting on an overcast and still day to cut down on wilting. If you don't have any choice and must plant on a sunny and/or windy day, then cover the transplants with a protective shield for a day or two. There are commercial blankets made of a nonwoven material that will do this and can also be used at night to protect against light frosts. A do-it-yourself way to provide shading is to form newspaper sheets into cones and place one over each plant, anchoring the edges with soil. Remove the cones after a day; by then the plants will be revived and will need the sun to help them grow vigorously.

Although starting your own boxed plants takes a bit of time and effort, it can be fun. As you watch tiny seedlings evolve into strong, healthy bedding plants, there is a real sense of renewal and accomplishment. Best of all, you can have as many plants as you want of exactly the species and varieties you prefer.

4 Planting Bedding Plants

Water bedding plants just before transplanting them into garden beds or planters to ensure that they slip out and separate easily. Pinch out the center growth bud to encourage bushiness. Turn the plants out of the pack and divide by pulling gently apart. Avoid excess damage to tender roots. Place the plant in a hole at the same depth or slightly deeper than it was in the pack. Firm the soil around the root with your fingers. Form a shallow dam around the plant to hold water—this is especially helpful if a flower bed is on a slope. Fill each dam with water that contains a weak fertilizer solution. This will get rid of air pockets around the roots and provide food to encourage quick growth.

Sowing Seeds

Sowing seeds directly into the garden is the simplest method of growing annuals. For those who have neither the extra money nor the inclination, proper facilities, or equipment to buy boxed plants, sowing directly into the garden in springtime is the answer. Once the ground is warm and the planting bed properly prepared, it's amazing how quickly most annuals sprout and grow to the flowering stage!

There are some plants that grow better when planted directly in the garden rather than started ahead as boxed plants. For example, zinnias experience difficulty surviving transplanting. You'll also find that trailing and vining plants can't be started very much ahead of planting out time or they become hopelessly entangled. As a result, most vines don't gain enough of a head start to make the extra effort worthwhile.

There are several ways to approach direct seeding. For a somewhat structured, but still informal cottage garden look, use a stick to mark out flowing sweeps on the prepared bed. Plant each sweep with a different kind of seed. If the garden is large enough to allow it, repeat the same variety in several sections. Place taller varieties toward the rear of the bed and the lower ones at the front. There is really no reason to precisely plan in advance where each kind will go.

Broadcast the seeds in each section and rake lightly, then briefly sprinkle a fine spray of water over the bed to settle the soil a bit. When the young seedlings sprout, they'll need to be thinned to prevent overcrowding. When thinning, adjust the space you leave between the plants according to their growth characteristics: Tall upright-growing plants such as feathered cockscomb, bachelor's buttons, and larkspur can be left much closer together than wide-spreading plants such as sweet alyssum, petunias, cosmos, and baby's breath. Surplus seedlings can be discarded, passed on to friends, or moved to grow in planters or other garden areas.

For a more formal garden design, make a precise plan on paper beforehand. Then carefully copy the layout onto the prepared seedbed. With this approach, each preselected variety is planted in rows or clumps in the appointed order—two or three seeds to a cluster, spaced 4 to 12 inches apart depending on their growth habits. When the plants are 1 to 2 inches tall,

Many annuals are easily started by seed outdoors.

thin out all but the strongest one from each cluster. The resulting beds will have a neat, organized, well-planned look that will enhance any formally laid-out garden design.

Another approach to flower bed layout is simply to mark off rows the length of the bed and plant each one with a different annual favorite. By planting the tallest kind in the back row and increasingly shorter ones in each row in front of it, it's possible to effectively display all varieties. Take into account the width to which each type grows when spacing the rows. Maintenance of this garden is easy because you always work along straight rows.

To decide which design style to use, consider what is best suited to your own tastes and talents, as well as to the style of your house and the already existing garden.

PLANTS TO START OUTDOORS

Sweet Alyssum*	Nasturtium
Baby's Breath	Ornamental Kale
Blanket Flower	Petunia
Coleus*	Phlox*
Cosmos*	California Poppy
Dahlia*	Portulaca
Forget-Me-Not	Sunflower
Gazania	Zinnia*
Marigold*	

*Those plants that might be started ahead indoors or bought as boxed bedding plants in Zone 5 and colder.

(Note: Some plants on this list also appear on the list of those that can be started ahead as boxed plants. Either option is acceptable.)

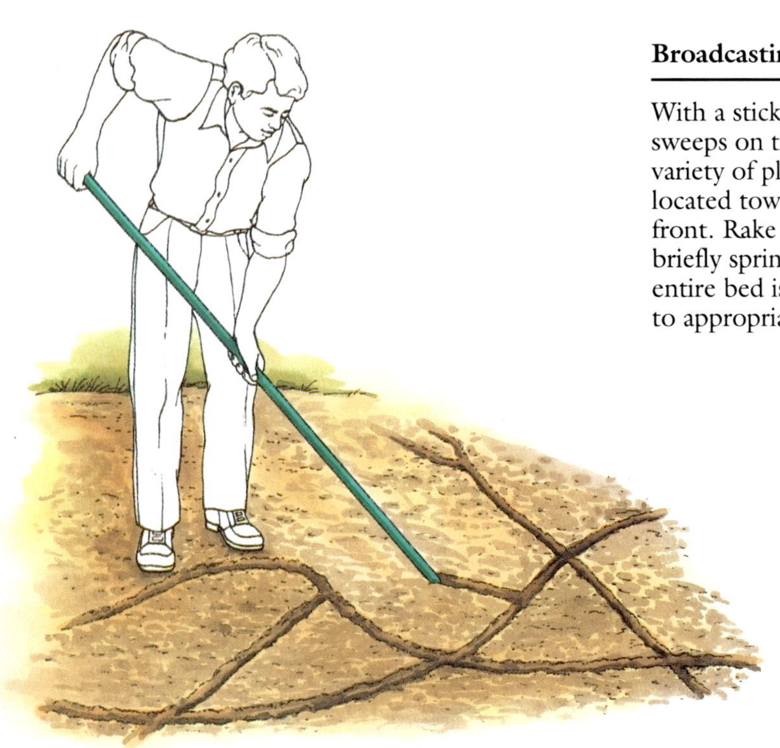

Broadcasting Seeds

With a stick or rake handle, mark out flowing abstract sweeps on the prepared bed. Broadcast a different variety of plant in each location, with taller types located toward the back and low-growing ones at the front. Rake the soil surface lightly after sowing, then briefly sprinkle with a fine spray of water after the entire bed is seeded. Seedlings will need to be thinned to appropriate spacing when they're 2 to 3 inches tall.

Planting Seeds over Mulch

For large plants that need to be spaced a foot or more apart, it's easiest to lay mulch over the bed prior to planting. Cut 3-inch holes at proper intervals in the mulch sheet. (If an organic mulch is used, push mulching aside for appropriate spacing.) Plant three seeds in a triangular pattern in each hole. Pat soil gently over each group. When seedlings grow their second set of leaves, thin out the weaker plants, leaving just the strongest one to continue growing.

Planting Seeds in Rows

Flower seeds planted in rows are easily cared for. If varieties are arranged so the tallest is in the back row with each row forward planted with a shorter variety, all of them will be visible from the front of the bed. Mulch can be laid in place before or after seed rows are sown. Thinning of seedlings for proper spacing should be done when plants are 2 to 3 inches high.

Propagating Stem Cuttings

Most annuals are grown from seeds. Although many perennials are started by other means such as root cuttings, stem cuttings, clump divisions, and so on, comparatively few annuals are reproduced asexually.

However, there are a few outstanding exceptions. Impatiens, fibrous begonias, coleus, and geraniums can all be easily grown from stem cuttings. When you want additional plants exactly like the mature plant in your garden and you want them to grow to blossoming size quickly, cuttings taken from the parent plant are the best way to accomplish this.

Select a mature plant in good health that is in a stage of active mid-summer growth. Don't wait until late summer when nights are shorter and cooler. By then, plant growth is slowing, making successful rooting more difficult.

Prepare a container filled with rooting medium. The container may be small or large, depending on how many cuttings you want to root. It should be at least 3 to 4 inches deep, filled with 2½ inches or more of rooting medium. Clean, coarse builder's sand is an old traditional rooting medium that still works well. A mixture of half perlite and half peat moss, or half perlite and half vermiculite, are other good choices. Fill the container with the moistened medium, then let it settle and drain for a half hour or more before inserting the cuttings.

Take cuttings in the morning when the parent plant is in top condition. Using a sharp knife, cut off growth tips just above the point where a leaf or side shoot attaches to the main stem—these points of attachment are called nodes. Each of the cuttings should be between 3 and 6 inches in length and have 4 to 6 nodes. The stem tissue should be succulent and easy to cut through; if it's woody and resistant to cutting, try again nearer the growing tip.

Don't spend more than five minutes taking cuttings from the parent plants. You want to get them indoors and replanted as quickly as possible to avoid loss of energy due to wilting. If you want to take more cuttings than are possible in that time period, bring the first group inside and plunge them into a container of cool water before going out to pick more.

To prepare a cutting for rooting, remove the leafless piece of stem at the bottom. Cut it off about ⅛ inch below the first node with a clean knife or razor cut, leaving no torn or dangling pieces of tissue hanging from the stem. Remove *all* of the leaves, complete with their leaf stems, from the lower half of the cutting. These can be cut off with a knife or manually snapped off. Do not leave any leaf portions attached because they can become sites at which destructive rot sets in.

Coleus plants are often grown from stem cuttings.

If there are any flower buds on the cutting, cut these off as well. If left, they'll drain away growth energy that's needed for root generation. Cut back the tips of any large leaves remaining on the cutting so that one-third to one-half of their surface remains. Some leaf area is needed to carry on conversion of sunlight into growth energy, but too much foliage will increase the possibility of wilting. It can also contribute to a fatal outbreak of fungus, a problem exacerbated by poor air circulation.

To help stimulate root formation, it's helpful, although not an absolute necessity, to coat the lower one-third of each stem cutting with rooting hormone powder. Just dip each stem in the rooting powder and tap the cutting lightly against the work surface to shake off any excess powder. Poke a hole in the dampened rooting medium, insert the cutting in the hole to one-third of its length, and press the medium firmly around the stem with your fingers. When all of the cuttings are set in the medium, water the surface to settle the rooting medium more closely around them.

Place a plastic bag over the cuttings and their container to form a tent, using bamboo stakes or wooden dowels as supports to hold the covering above the cuttings. This will serve as a mini-greenhouse, which should be kept out of direct sunlight. It will also maintain a high moisture level that will keep the cuttings from wilting.

If the bottom edge of the plastic tent is left a bit loose, some fresh outside air will be able to circulate up inside. This will help reduce the possibility of mildew and mold problems. Some growers prefer to hold the plastic tightly against the container with an elastic band. In this case, it's necessary to remove the elastic and lift up the tent sides for a short period each day or else to poke holes in the plastic bag in order to supply the cutting with necessary fresh air.

With a plastic tent there will be little, if any, need for watering the cuttings. Water within the tent will evaporate during the heat of the day, then condense again at night. If the rooting medium seems dry when rolled between the fingers, water should be added sparingly.

Succulent annual cuttings will root quickly. They should be checked in a week to ten days. Insert a narrow knife blade or a fork beneath one of the cuttings and gently lift it out. When the longest roots are ¼ inch long, remove cuttings from the rooting medium and transfer each to a 1- to 1½-inch pot filled with planting mix. Do *not* transplant into pots larger than this even if you ultimately want to grow the plants in larger groups. Small plants survive better and grow faster when placed in small pots first and are later moved into larger pots when their systems are larger.

These new plants can be grown as potted plants to be enjoyed indoors over winter. In turn, they can be used as parent plants from which to take cuttings to root and grow in the garden the following summer.

Propagating Healthy Plants from Stem Cuttings

1 Cut 3- to 6-inch growth tips from the parent plant with a small, sharp paring knife. Make a clean, slanted cut just above a leaf node, side shoot, or growth bud.

2 Bring the cutting indoors immediately. Recut the stems just below the bottom node. Use a single-edged razor blade or a sharp paring knife to give the cleanest possible cut. A cutting is ready to plant after the side shoots and leaves have been removed from the lower half of the stem. Any flowers or flower buds should also be removed, and large leaves trimmed back to about half their original size. Dip the lower one-third to one-half of the stem in rooting powder. Tap off any excess powder.

3 Poke a hole in the rooting medium and insert a cutting to between one-third and one-half of its length. Firm the rooting medium around the stem with your fingers. When all the cuttings are inserted, water them in place. A large, clear plastic bag forms a mini-greenhouse over the cuttings. The bag is held several inches above the tops of the cuttings by sticks or stakes inserted around the edge of the container.

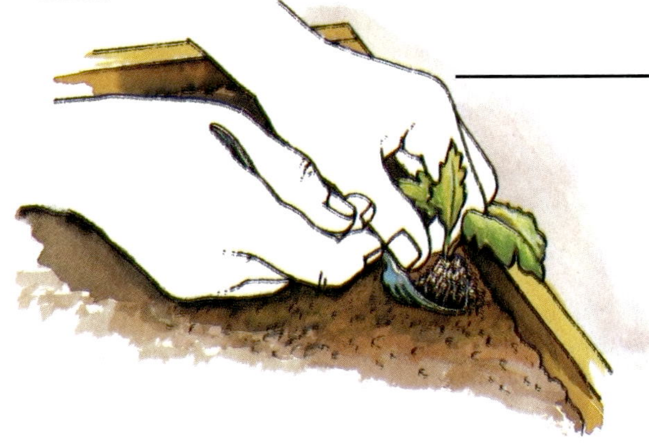

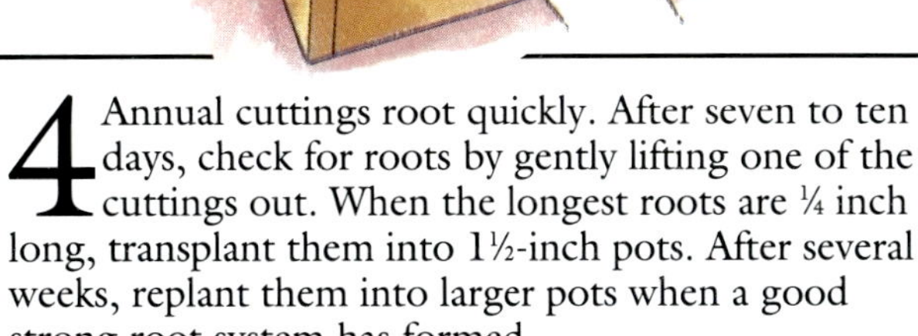

4 Annual cuttings root quickly. After seven to ten days, check for roots by gently lifting one of the cuttings out. When the longest roots are ¼ inch long, transplant them into 1½-inch pots. After several weeks, replant them into larger pots when a good strong root system has formed.

Caring for Annuals

Quenching a Plant's Thirst

Along with soil and light, water is an essential ingredient for plant growth. The soil and light requirements of annuals have been dealt with on page 6; the ways to take care of their water needs will now be considered.

It's not easy, especially at first, to gauge exactly when plants require water—so much depends upon current weather and soil conditions. For example, if good soaking rains fall frequently, it's obvious additional watering is unnecessary. However, when there's a light rainfall every few days, it's possible that only the soil surface has been dampened without much water actually reaching plant roots, necessitating the addition of water. Plants subjected to bright sun and wind also lose a lot of water that needs to be replenished. Similarly, because trees continually pull large quantities of moisture from the surrounding soil, annuals planted near or under them need more frequent watering than those in the open. All of these factors affect the rate at which soil dries out.

So how do you judge when to water and how much water to give? The one sure way to test is by poking your finger 2 to 3 inches into the soil and feeling how moist or dry it is. Taking a pinch from the surface isn't good enough; you need to know what it's like down in the root zone. Inexperienced gardeners should check soil moisture any day that there is little or no rainfall. Over time, you'll develop a feel for the overall conditions and check only when you suspect the soil may be turning dry. Remember, it's always better to check too often rather than not often enough. Don't wait until drooping plants indicate that the soil is parched.

When you do water, water deeply. Many people briefly spray a thirsty flower bed with a hand-held hose. When they tire of holding it, become bored, or think they have watered enough because the water has stopped soaking into the soil as rapidly as it did at first, the watering session is ended. Always pause to check how deeply the water has penetrated. Guessing usually results in reaching only the top ½ inch, leaving the soil beneath it still dry.

Deeply watered annuals are usually very healthy.

A better approach is to use an automatic sprinkler, letting it gently "rain" for an extended period of time. Check at half-hour intervals to see how deeply the water has penetrated. Turn the water off when the soil is moistened to a 2-inch depth. Don't water again until your testing indicates the need.

One problem with sprinkler water is that the foliage becomes very wet, creating an ideal environment for the spread of fungus diseases. In addition, flower clusters heavy with water are more likely to bend and break or to become mildewed.

The best way to water is with a soaker hose. The water slowly oozes from the hose's many tiny holes for several hours—even overnight. All of the water soaks directly on the soil and down to the plant roots without any waste or damage. Drip irrigation is another excellent slow-soaking system, but it's more expensive than a soaker hose. Thus it's probably a sensible alternative only for those who have large plant beds or who garden in climates where irrigation is constantly needed in order for cultivated plants to survive. Once the system is permanently laid out, it can remain in place year after year; in areas that freeze, however, it must be drained for the winter.

There are two additional factors that will help conserve moisture and thus reduce the frequency of need for watering. One is the incorporation of peat moss into the planting area; this causes the soil to be able to soak up and hold water longer. (This is true when peat is added to light and sandy soils; conversely, when it's added to heavy soils, it helps to lighten and aerate them.)

The second technique that helps retain moisture is the use of mulch. Laid on the soil surface between the plants, a mulch protects the soil from sun and wind drying. (More on the benefits of mulch, as well as descriptions of various mulch alternatives, can be found in the following section, "Keeping Weeds at Bay.")

By using these two ideas, you can cut down on the time needed to care for your garden, and even more importantly, help conserve water, nature's precious resource.

Soaker Hose Watering

An easy way to handle deep watering of an annuals bed is to lay a soaker hose in place when plants are small and leave it there for the season. Mulch can be laid on top of the soaker hose without disruption. A quick connector on the soaker hose allows speedy attachment to the regular garden hose whenever watering is needed. When soil is well-soaked, the garden hose can easily be disconnected and stored out of the way until it's needed again.

The Benefits of Deep Watering

When plants are watered infrequently but heavily, they'll develop large and deep root networks. Frequent light waterings cause plants to develop shallow root systems just below the soil surface. This causes plants to be poorly anchored and therefore subject to toppling in heavy wind or rain, as well as liable to wilting unless they're watered daily. Therefore, slow, deep-soak watering produces stronger and hardier plants. Whenever possible, water in the evening or overnight rather than in the morning or in the heat of the day.

Plants with Water Dams

A dam of soil ringed around each plant when it's transplanted into the garden helps to keep the water from settling in and early rains from running off immediately. This gives the water time to soak in around the plant's roots. Where flower beds are level, this isn't essential, but when planting on a slope, a dam is a great help. The dam disappears after a week or two and is no longer needed.

Watering with a Drip Irrigation System

For very large planting beds or in very dry or sandy conditions, a drip irrigation system may be the best watering solution. It allows slow, deep watering directly into each plant's roots. This helps keep foliage dry, thus reducing the possibility of the spread of diseases. Use this system in conjunction with a mulch for greatest water conservation. An on-off timer and a soluble fertilizer feeder are optional parts of a drip-irrigation system for those wanting the additional ease of maintenance they allow.

Keeping Weeds at Bay

The gardening chore everyone likes least is weeding. Luckily, there are several good ways in which to reduce the need for this often disliked gardening chore.

The old traditional approaches are to regularly pull the weeds up, chop them off below ground level with a hoe, or claw them out with a cultivator. These are still perfectly good ways to deal with weeds. In addition, though, there are several techniques for actually reducing the number of weeds requiring removal.

Weed seeds are quick to germinate and grow rapidly once they do. As soon as they're brought to within an inch of the soil surface (through digging), they'll begin to sprout. Seeds deeper in the soil will remain dormant. We can take advantage of this characteristic. After digging deeply in early spring to ready the bed for planting, wait a week or more before doing any planting or seed sowing. Every three days, stir up the top 1 inch of soil with a scuffle hoe or cultivator, leaving the lower soil undisturbed. This will expose several cycles of young, sprouted weeds to dry out and die in the sun and air. If care is then taken not to dig deeper than 1 inch when sowing your garden seeds, few of the competitor weeds will remain. This approach can be used when seeds are going to be planted either in addition to, or instead of, bedding plants. But in places where *only* bedding plants will be used, another type of weed control is gaining popularity—the use of a pre-emergent chemical. This is sprinkled on the soil around the already planted annuals. It's important that the annuals be at least 3 to 4 inches tall before the chemical, triluralin, is applied. In the case of seedlings, this same chemical can be applied once the young plants have grown to this 3- to 4-inch size, but no earlier in their growth cycle.

Finally, the most popular way of dramatically reducing weed problems is by using some kind of mulch. Mulch is a layer of organic or inorganic material laid on the soil surface to shade out weeds, retain soil moisture, and have a moderating effect on soil temperature.

Many materials can achieve these results, but some are more practical, less expensive, easier to handle, and much more attractive than others. Availability of some mulching materials also varies in different parts of the country. The list of organic mulches includes pine needles, leaves, straw, dried seaweed, tree bark strips, bark chunks, peat moss, old newspapers, sawdust, wood chips, cocoa bean hulls, and cotton seed hulls. Inorganic mulches include "blankets" made from solid sheets of black plastic (**Caution:** These can become very slippery when wet); black plastic made porous with thousands of small holes; porous, non-woven fiberglass landscape fabric; and pieces of new or used carpets. What you choose will depend primarily upon personal preference, cost, and availability.

Mulching helps curb the growth of weeds.

Perhaps the choice of which kind of mulch to use isn't as important as the decision to use *some* kind of mulch. Mulching cuts down dramatically on weed problems, conserves soil moisture, keeps soil warmer in cool weather and cooler on hot days, and, if it's an organic mulch, will improve the quality of the soil as it breaks down and adds to what gardeners call "soil tilth."

With so many advantages to offer, mulches are one of the best gardening "tools" available. Naturally, there are also a few disadvantages. Some mulches are not very attractive-looking (but may be used as a weed and moisture barrier and be covered with a thin layer of some better-looking material—pebbles or straw laid over black plastic, for example). Other organic mulches may alter the soil chemistry as they break down (annual soil tests will detect these changes so you can adjust fertilizer applications to compensate). Still other types have an odor when they're fresh or may prove too expensive for use in large quantities.

Still, there must be at least one among all of the alternatives that will satisfy your needs. The use of a mulch will dramatically reduce weed problems in any garden. The few that do appear can easily be removed by direct pulling.

Using a Pre-Emergent Chemical

Granules of a pre-emergent chemical can be scattered on the soil between the already planted bedding plants. It will prevent weed seeds from sprouting in these open areas. Because it kills *all* seeds—weeds, annuals, and perennials—do *not* use a pre-emergent in any area where you have recently planted, or plan to plant, flower seeds. A pre-emergent can be used once seedlings have germinated and grown to bedding plant size or larger.

Seedlings and Mulch

Where seeds are to be planted instead of bedding plants, wait to lay in organic mulches until they've germinated and the seedlings are 3 inches or taller. This reduces possible smothering of vulnerable, young seedlings by mulch that the wind may blow over them. Watering down of organic mulches after they're laid helps settle and hold them in place.

Boxed Plants and Mulching

Mulch, whether organic or inorganic, can be laid before planting of boxed plants. Holes can be cut through sheeting or dug through organic mulches at proper spacing for the plants.

Cultivation of Nonmulched Areas

In beds where no mulch is used, frequent cultivation of the top 1 to 2 inches of soil is the best way to control weeds. Newly germinated weed seedlings die quickly when stirred up this way. Larger weeds should be hand-pulled and removed from the bed, since they can easily reroot if left in the garden.

Feeding Alternatives

Every nursery and garden center offers numerous plant foods. There are sacks of organic fertilizers such as dried cow manure, dried blood, and bonemeal, as well as inorganic commercial fertilizers (nitrogen, phosphorus, and potassium in various formulas—5-10-5, 10-10-10, 11-8-7, etc.). Shelves are filled with boxes and bottles of nearly every nitrogen-phosphorus-potassium (NPK) formula imaginable, along with the old standby—organic fish emulsion.

Manufacturers have developed special fertilizer blends that they advertise as best for roses, fruit trees, vegetables, or garden flowers. Unfortunately, all this abundance causes confusion. What is best for your needs?

As mentioned in "Soil and Light" found on page 6, the best course to follow is to have your garden soil tested each year, then follow the recommendations given with your test results. Any other approach invites problems of supplying excessive amounts of some nutrients and too little of others.

Knowing what nutrients are needed helps cut down on the number of choices, but still leaves the decision of whether to use an organic or inorganic source up to you. If you're able to obtain the nutrients you need from organic fertilizers, you reduce the risk of possibly harming the environment through overfeeding. However, if the nutrients you require cannot realistically be obtained from such sources, there's little danger in using inorganic fertilizers as long as you apply only as much as is needed. The problems caused by inorganic fertilizers are primarily due to careless usage.

As you study the NPK formula on each plant food, you'll notice that organic fertilizers contain much lower percentages of nutrients per pound than do inorganic fertilizers. For the most part, this doesn't matter when feeding annuals. If the formula is half strength, for example, you can feed twice as often—four weekly feedings rather than two feedings two weeks apart—and the plants will obtain the same amount of nutrients.

Where this *can* become a problem is when you're trying to adjust a large garden bed's nutrient content at the beginning of the growing season, especially if it hasn't been fertilized in years. You may find that, in order to raise the nutrients to the recommended level, you'll have to add 4 inches of the organic material. This

Fertilizers help provide nutrients to healthy annuals.

can be done if the area to be covered is small, but for large areas, it could become unwieldy. In these cases it's more practical to make major adjustments with inorganic foods, then proceed with organics for minor adjustments in future years.

Fertilizers are applied in a dry granular or powder form, or mixed with water for a liquid application. The granular or powder foods should be broadcasted over the soil surface and dug in; liquid applications can be made with a hand sprayer or a special mixing attachment for your garden hose.

To supply food for immediate use by bedding annuals that are newly planted out, a weak solution of water soluble fertilizer—either fish emulsion or an inorganic type—can be poured from a watering can directly around each plant to help get it off to a good start. Thereafter, a couple of sidedressings of granular plant food sprinkled around each plant at two-week intervals should nicely carry them through the rest of the summer.

For best absorption, fertilize when the soil is moist. Take care to apply it on the soil rather than on the plant leaves. If you do inadvertently get it on the plants, hose them off with water within the hour to avoid chemical burning of the leaves. The plants, your hands, and the fertilizer should be dry when you fertilize. **Caution:** Always wash your hands after handling fertilizer.

A final word regarding two homemade soil amenders: compost and liquid manure. Compost is made by combining plant wastes with soil and fertilizer, allowing them to decompose for several months, then mixing them back into the garden. Liquid manure is made by combining animal wastes and water, allowing them to decompose, then watering the garden with the resultant liquid. Both are good organic nutrient sources for those interested in producing them even though their level of nutrients is low. However, neither is especially practical for the average, small-home garden. Most gardeners will find it more convenient to purchase fish emulsion and bagged compost at their garden shop.

Making Organic Fertilizer

Gardeners preferring organic fertilizers can make their own liquid manure by fermenting animal and vegetable wastes in water for several weeks. An easy and reliable source of soluble organic fertilizer is fish emulsion, which can be purchased at any garden center. When adding this concentrate to water, there is a strong fish odor. Therefore, it's best to do this job outdoors or in a well-ventilated area. Fortunately, the odor is very short-lived.

Composting

Making your own compost from plant wastes, soil, and nutrients takes several months. Many gardeners find it easier to purchase bagged compost rather than to make their own. Either way, compost is a good additive for soils low in organic materials.

Sidedressing

Granular and powdered commercial fertilizers release nutrients more quickly than organic fertilizers. Sprinkling a small handful of 5-10-5 or 10-10-10 around each plant (known as sidedressing) in late spring and again in mid-summer will give annuals a feeding boost that will keep them in top growing and flowering condition on through the summer.

Liquid Fertilizer Solution

Another fast source of nutrients is a liquid fertilizer solution. This comes in a concentrated form that is then diluted by mixing with water according to the manufacturer's directions. Use a mild solution in water in newly planted bedding plants or recently thinned seedlings to help them quickly recover from the shock. Liquid fertilizer can also be applied in place of powdered or granular sidedressings, if preferred.

Ways to Increase/Control Growth

As has already been described, annuals will flourish when provided with the best possible growing conditions. However, there are a few simple care techniques that will help increase and control their growth. These, in turn, will increase the abundance of color in your summer garden.

PINCHING BACK—To encourage plants to fill out, remove the growth bud at the end of the main stem when the plant is in its rapid growth stage that precedes first flower bud formation. For bedding plants, the best time to do this is when you're planting them out in the garden. They're at a good stage of growth and, in addition, the removal of some of their foliage will help balance any root damage they may suffer in the transplanting process. Plants grown from seeds sown directly in the garden should be pinched back when they're 3 to 4 inches tall.

DEADHEADING—Once annuals begin to bloom, it's important to remove spent flowers promptly for several reasons. First, once the flower dies, it detracts from the good looks of the garden. Second, even though we say it's dead, it's actually very much alive and continues with its growth toward seed production. This process pulls plant energy that would otherwise be available for new foliage and flower production into the seed head. Third, removal of spent flowers helps to quickly redirect plant energy to side shoots for smooth and speedy transfer to new growth.

Occasionally it becomes necessary to cut back growth in order to keep a plant from becoming leggy or from drowning out neighboring plants. Cutting back should be approached in the same way as removing dead flower heads. Always cut back to a side growth shoot or branch that is headed in the direction you want future growth to go. This way you can steer and control growth as you see fit.

STAKING—Most healthy annuals are sturdy and self-supporting. They often don't require any special staking to keep them looking good. However, plants with heavy flower clusters, especially those on tall, slender stems such as snapdragons and dahlias, may flop over when exposed to strong winds or heavy rains. Another group that sometimes requires support to keep their flower heads visible are those with stems that will either bend over or break off when the weight of their leaves and blooms becomes too great. Asters, baby's breath, and some zinnias are known to have these problems.

These dahlias are staked for better growth.

Often plants gain enough support when a kind of corral is placed around them. The plant stems lean out against the metal or string sides of the corral instead of flopping down to the ground. Another simple type of support consists of poking many-branched pieces of brush into the ground beside the plants. These form a network of twigs through which the plants can grow and against which they can lean for support. The tops of these branches can be bent over to form an even more interlaced network if needed.

These two support systems work well with plants that have a spreading growth habit. For those that produce tall, single spikes, a third staking method is more suitable. Poke a wooden or bamboo stake into the ground 2 to 3 inches from the plant stem. It should be pushed deeply enough into the soil to be solidly secure. Loosely tie each plant stem to this central stake every 6 inches along the stem's height. A final tie should be made just below the flower bud cluster. To keep the ties from sliding downward, first form a half-granny knot around the stake, then a full granny knot around the plant stem.

Pinching out Growth Tips

Pinching out the plant growth tip helps encourage multiple branching. This, in turn, causes production of more flower buds along these additional branches. At the same time, pinching produces a more sturdy, compact plant that not only looks nice but is also less subject to breakage due to wind, rain, or heavy bloom weight.

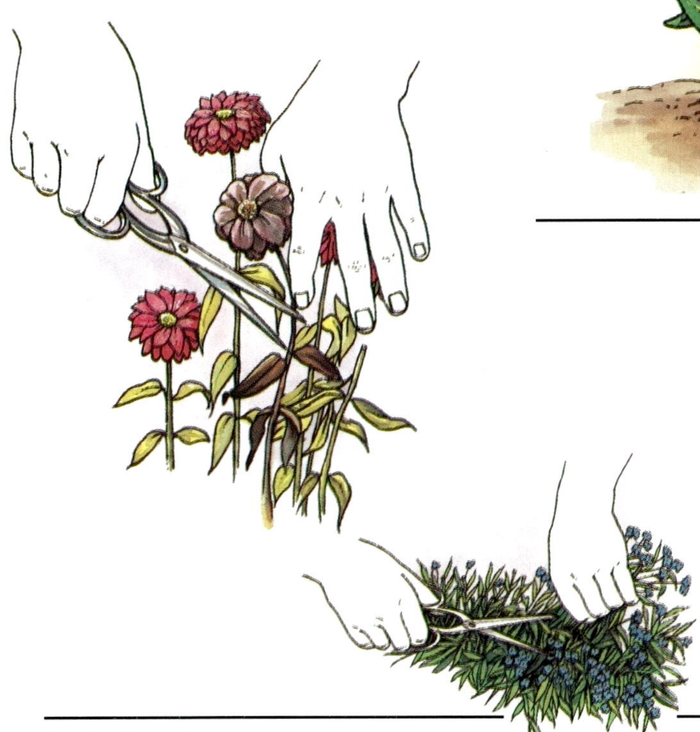

Deadheading Flower Heads

Deadheading, or removing dead flower heads, should be done soon after the flower dies, so no plant energy is wasted on seed formation. Cluster flowers will look fresh and attractive longer if the individual florets are snapped out of the group as they die. Single flowers should be cut back to the place on the stem where a side shoot is already pushing out. If none are evident, then cut back to above a leaf, a node, or a side branch. Cut on a slant to allow water to run off of the wound.

Stake Corrals

A good way to hold clumps of fine stems upright is by inserting four or more stakes around the plant. Tie a string to the first stake, then wrap it one turn around each of the other stakes around the perimeter and back to the starter stake. For a large clump, run string diagonally across within this corral for more support. Several tiers of string may be needed for tall plants—space tiers 4 to 6 inches apart. Flower heads should float 4 to 6 inches above the top tier of strings.

Brush Thicket Staking

A simple no-cost plant support for fine-stemmed annuals can be made by poking the stems of well-branched brush into the ground next to the young plants. The plants' stems simply lean against the twigs for support without any tying. This brush thicket will give even more support if the tops are bent over and interwoven. Plant stems will grow up through the resulting tangle and hide it from view.

Pests and Other Problems

The following lists are designed to help you identify the most common garden pests and diseases. However, if you feel uncertain about what is causing damage to your plants, it is advisable that you take a specimen to your local garden shop or your county Cooperative Extension office to have it identified.

Once you know what your problem is, you'll need to decide how to control it. When an infestation is slight, it's often possible to simply remove the sick plants or individual insects. For a heavy infestation, you'll probably need to turn to chemical insecticides or fungicides.

Just remember to follow manufacturer's instructions precisely, and to read and follow any cautions on the package label.

Healthy flowers and foliage make for attractive gardens.

INSECTS AND ANIMALS

SYMPTOM	CAUSE	CURE	PLANTS
Cluster of small, soft-bodied insects on buds and growth tips (gray, black, pink, or green in color); sticky secretions may be evident	Aphids	Spray with rotenone or malathion[1] in evening.	Pot Marigold Nasturtium Primrose
Leaves chewed away; hard-shelled beetles on plant and burrowed into flowers	Beetles of various kinds	Spray with rotenone or Sevin*[1]; pick by hand and destroy.	Hollyhock American/French Marigold Zinnia
Growth tips wilted; small hole in plant stem at point where wilting begins	Borer	Snap off at level of hole, dig out borer and destroy; spray with endosulfan[1], pyrethrum, or rotenone.	American/French Marigold Zinnia

[1] = Inorganic treatment

* = Copyrighted brand name.

INSECTS AND ANIMALS (continued)

SYMPTOM	CAUSE	CURE	PLANTS
Leaves and flowers chewed away; caterpillars on plant	Caterpillars of various kinds and sizes	Pick off by hand and destroy; spray with pyrethrum, malathion[1], or *Bacillus thuringiensis.*	Nicotiana Ornamental/ Flowering Cabbage Petunia
Entire young plants wilted; partially or entirely chewed through at ground level	Cutworms	Dig in soil around plant base; find rolled up caterpillars and destroy; circle plant with cardboard collar (1" below ground and 1" above ground).	China Pink Nicotiana Ornamental/ Flowering Cabbage Petunia
Leaves and stems chewed; insects seen hopping and flying	Grasshoppers	Spray with Sevin*[1]; pick off by hand.	Petunia
Leaves peppered with small, round holes; small, triangular-shaped bugs seen when disturbed	Leaf Hoppers	Spray with malathion[1] or methozychlor[1]; dust with diatomaceous earth.	Aster Dahlia Pot Marigold
Leaves "painted" with whitish, curling trails	Leaf Miners	Spray with malathion[1]; remove and destroy badly infested leaves.	China Pink Hollyhock
Plants entirely gone or eaten down to small stubs; evidence of footprints or droppings	Rabbits or Deer	Spray with Hinder*[1]; fence out rabbits with 3'- high chicken wire or other close-woven fencing.	Impatiens Ornamental Cabbage/Kale Pansy
Silvery slime trails plants; soft sticky slugs on plants after dark (check with flashlight)	Slugs and Snails	Set out shallow containers of beer; set out metaldehyde slug bait[1]; pick by hand after dark or on dark days.	Hollyhock Nicotiana Petunia Primrose
Leaves yellowing with speckled look; fine spider webs on backs of leaves and at point where leaves attach to stem; very tiny bugs on backs of leaves	Spider Mites	Spray with a miticide[1] from underneath to hit backs of leaves; wash or spray with soapy water.	Impatiens Primrose

INSECTS AND ANIMALS (continued)

SYMPTOM	CAUSE	CURE	PLANTS
Small glob of white bubbles on plant stem or leaves; small insect hidden inside	Spittlebug	Ignore unless very pervasive; spray with malathion[1]; wash off repeatedly with water from hose.	Bachelor's Button

DISEASES

SYMPTOM	CAUSE	CURE	PLANTS
Leaves become mottled, curl, and shrivel; plants become deformed	Blights and Viruses	Remove and destroy plants; buy blight-resistant strains; do not smoke; wash hands before handling plants.	Aster Snapdragon
Newly sprouted seedlings fall over and die	Damping Off	Start seeds in sterile soil mix. Dust seeds with Captan*[1] before planting.	All plants
Round, dusty brown or black spots on leaves; leaves drop from plant	Leaf Spot	Remove badly diseased leaves and destroy; spray with benomyl[1] or zineb[1].	Aster Phlox
Lower leaves and stems turn grayish and look slightly wilted	Powdery Mildew	Increase air circulation; spray with benomyl[1] or sulfur.	Bachelor's Button Floss Flower Phlox Zinnia
Orange or reddish-brown raised dots form on backs of leaves; leaves look wilted	Rust	Increase air circula-ation; keep foliage dry; buy rust-resistant varieties; spray with ferbam[1] or zineb[1]; spray flowers with sulfur or benomyl.	Cleome Hollyhock Snapdragon
Leaves wilt and turn yellow; entire plant shuts down and dies	Wilt	Remove infected plants and destroy; buy wilt-resistant varieties.	Aster Dahlia Snapdragon

[1] = Inorganic treatment

* = Copyrighted brand name.

Gardening with Annuals

Laying Out an Annuals Garden

It is seldom possible to create an attractive annuals garden simply by planting out boxed plants or flower seeds without any plan. More often than not, this approach will produce unsatisfactory results. You need advance planning. Without it, it's easy to slip up and be disappointed. The best way to plan is with a simple sketch. Draw a quick outline of your garden bed, noting down its approximate dimensions and the amount of sun the area receives each day. Also list the names of your favorite annuals so you'll be sure to include most, if not all, of them in your plan.

The next step is to look up your favorites and to note the colors they come in and their growth habits. Mark down whether they prefer full sun, partial shade, or full shade. Also specify how tall they grow (T=tall, I=intermediate, L=low, V=vining). Check to see if any of your favorites prefer a different amount of sun from what your site has available; cross out those that aren't suitable. In other words, if you love impatiens, but your bed is in full sun, only New Guinea impatiens will succeed there. (Since other varieties of impatiens do not tolerate full sun, you may want to see if there's a shady location elsewhere in the yard or on a covered porch where you can enjoy a few instead.)

Mixing annuals and vegetables is a popular gardening idea.

ANNUALS FOR MIXED GARDENS

Sweet Alyssum	Nasturtium
Aster	Nicotiana
Baby's Breath	Pansy
Bachelor's Button	Petunia
Cockscomb	Phlox
Coleus	Portulaca
Cosmos	Salvia
Dahlia	Snapdragon
Forget-Me-Not	Verbena
Hollyhock	Vinca
Impatiens	Xeranthemum
Larkspur	Zinnia
Lisianthus	
American/French Marigold	

If you have very few favorites and a large space to fill, add a second list of annuals that you find attractive and that fit the light and color limitations of your site. Use seed catalogs to help choose the variety of petunia, marigold, snapdragon, or whatever, with the color and height you want. Be sure to note down several variety names and sources if a plant comes in more than one desirable color.

For those with limited garden space, a mixed garden makes good sense. It allows you to have some personal favorites, rather than limiting you to only a few kinds of plants—as is the case of massed garden designs.

A mixed garden is a very personal one that truly reflects the individual taste of the homeowners. Rather than being a garden for show, it's a garden designed for the pleasure of those who own it. If others who visit it also find it enjoyable, so much the better.

Some uniquely charming mixed gardens are possible. Fruit trees, such as peach, pear, or apple, can supply partial shade to flower beds filled with combinations of different-colored annuals and perennials. Clumps of favorite vegetables can also be placed among these flowering plants. The casual visitor might never notice these, since so many vegetables have attractive foliage to add to the garden scene. Feathery carrot tops, purplish beet greens, the bold and interesting foliage of parsnips, smooth, blue-green onion spikes, and large rhubarb leaves all make attractive additions to any flower bed.

Use colored pencils to color in planting sections within your bed outline. A more informal and interesting design will result if you vary the size and shape of these sections. Then decide which plants should go into what sections of your plan. Remember to keep tall plants in the back and low plants up front, filling in with intermediate heights. That way none of the plants will be blocked from view. If a bed is going to be in an area where it will be seen from all sides, the tallest plants should be in the center of the bed with low ones around the outer edges.

As you plan, be sure flower colors in adjacent sections vary but don't clash. Maintain a balance of color in the bed—avoid placing all the same-colored flowered plants on one side. In large beds, repeat the same variety in several sections, making the sections much larger than you would in smaller beds.

Once the plan is in its final form, you can then figure out approximately how many plants you'll need of each kind to fill the allotted space. This will help in ordering seeds for sowing or starting ahead and in buying boxed bedding plants.

Annuals Garden Against a Wall or Fence

This plan shows how to lay out a garden bed so all of the plants will be well displayed against the backdrop of a wall, fence, or building. Note that space has been left between the wall and the rear of the flower bed so gardening work—weeding, watering, spraying, etc.—can be done from both sides of the bed.

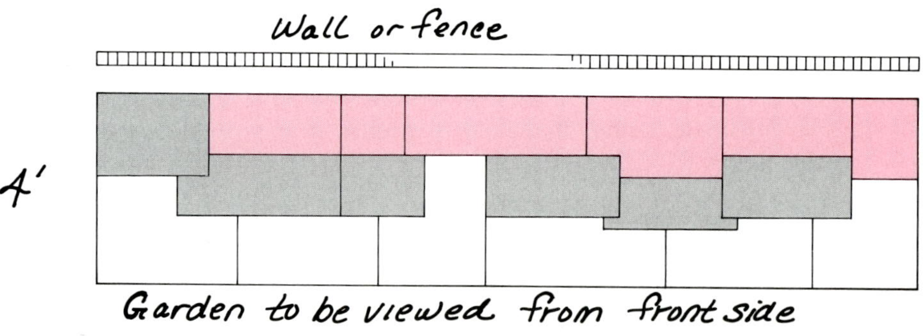

Annuals Garden Displayed from All Sides

When planting a flower bed that is to be on display from all sides, the plants should be placed as illustrated in this plan. A pathway through the middle of the bed allows easy access for plant care if a bed is wider than 3 to 4 feet.

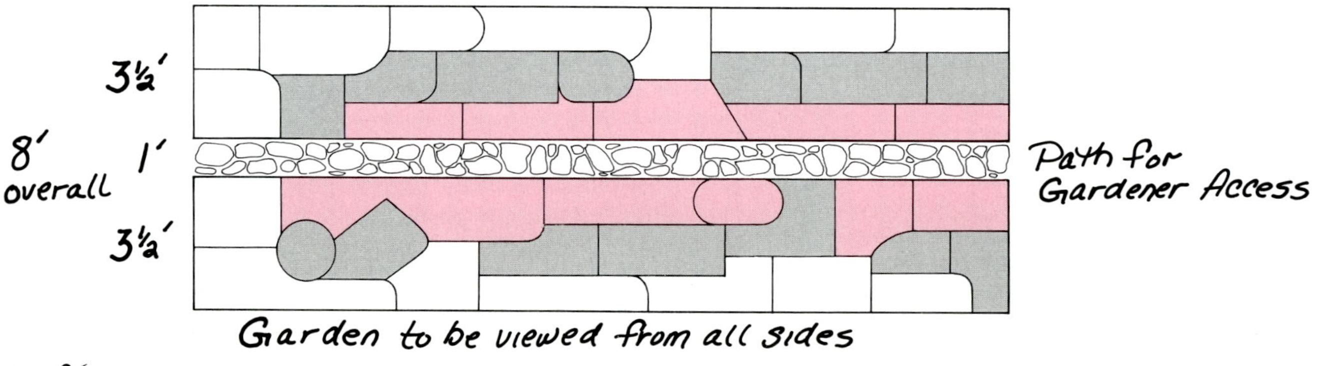

Combining Annuals, Fruits, and Vegetables

This small garden contains a mixture of annuals, fruits, and vegetables. The plan could easily be modified to include your own food favorites.

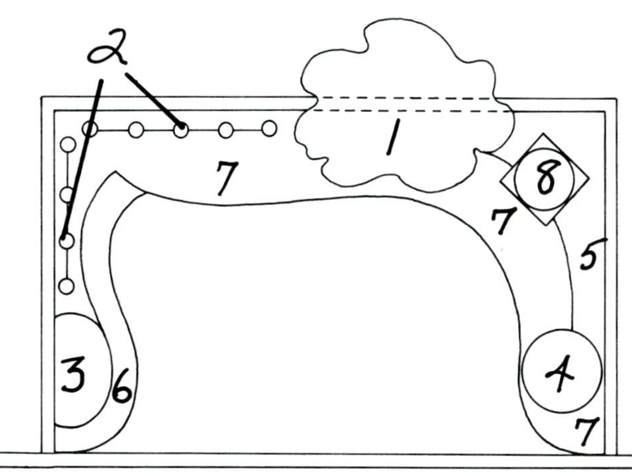

1. Favorite flowering tree
2. Pole beans, snap peas, or raspberries on trellis
3. Rhubarb
4. Blueberry (2 different varieties for cross-pollination)
5. Beets or Swiss chard
6. Herbs and other vegetable favorites
7. Flowering annuals
8. Fountain, statue, or other garden feature

Container Gardening

Probably no form of gardening allows more versatility than container gardening. Growing plants in containers makes it possible to garden in situations where there is no yard or soil available: on a rooftop, a high-rise balcony, a deck, a fire escape, or even in an area that's covered with concrete.

The containers themselves can be as plain or elaborate as you wish. Clay or plastic pots; wood, plastic, or metal window boxes; decorator pots of ceramic, terra cotta, alabaster, or wrought iron; recycled plastic or metal pails; wire frames lined with sphagnum moss; a child's cast-off metal wagon; hanging planters; a plastic-lined bushel basket—any of these can be used. Here's a chance to give your imagination free rein!

All that's essential is that the container be capable of holding soil as well as allowing excess water to drain away. Keep in mind that plants thrive more readily in larger amounts of soil because the soil temperature and moisture level fluctuate less as soil volume increases. Unless the gardener is extremely vigilant, plants are more likely to suffer frequent drying out and overheating when planted in small pots.

Annuals are particularly well-suited for use in container plantings. They quickly fill and overflow the planters. You can also plant them in masses of a single species or in a mixture of different kinds and colors.

Another advantage to growing plants in containers is their portability. You can move them from one area to another at will, as long as you remember that shade-loving plants can quickly burn if shifted into brilliant sun. Conversely, sun lovers won't flourish if shaded for more than a few days.

ANNUALS THAT DO WELL IN CONTAINERS

Fibrous Begonia	Pot Marigold
Coleus	Nasturtium
Geranium	Pansy
Impatiens	Petunia
Lobelia	Phlox
American/French Marigold	Verbena
	Vinca

Annuals are particularly suited for container gardening.

Planters full of annuals can be used singly or in groups. They can be mixed with houseplants brought outdoors for summer or inserted here and there in between shrubbery. Container plants can be hung from a garden fence, a low-hanging tree limb, or a porch rail. Even a small apartment balcony can be turned into a colorful garden by filling it with annuals.

Care of container plantings takes little total time, but it does require daily attention. Soil moisture needs to be checked every evening. When the weather is dry and windy, you may even need to check soil moisture morning and evening. Rub a small amount of the surface soil from each pot between your thumb and finger to test the moisture level. Ideally, you want to rewater each planter *before* the soil becomes bone dry. On the other hand, the soil should not be constantly soaking wet or the plants will drown. Therefore, it's necessary to keep track of the moisture level very conscientiously.

To be sure that water reaches all of the soil in the container, fill the planter to the rim with water allowing it to soak in completely. If no water comes out of the drainage holes, fill again. Repeat this process until water starts to drip from the bottom of the container.

To keep the plantings looking full and to encourage abundant blooming, remove dead flower heads promptly. At the same time, check for any signs of insect or disease problems. Once every 10 days to two weeks, water with a mild fertilizer solution. That's all it takes to keep container gardens in peak condition.

Container gardening can be an ideal solution for people with physical limitations that prevent them from working down at ground level. It can also be the answer for those with soil problems. For anyone, growing annuals in containers can provide an extra dimension of gardening pleasure, both outdoors in summer and indoors in winter.

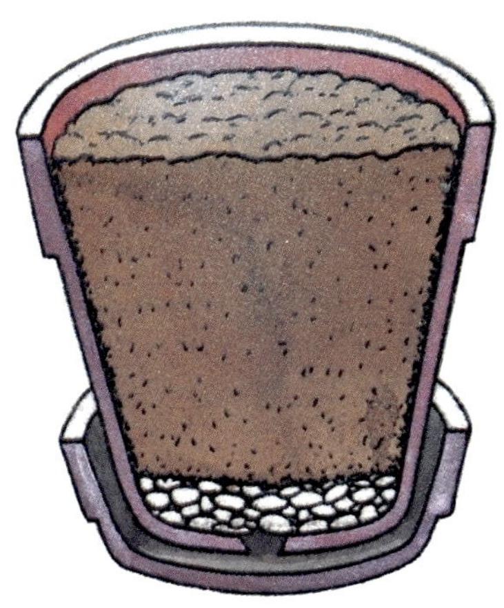

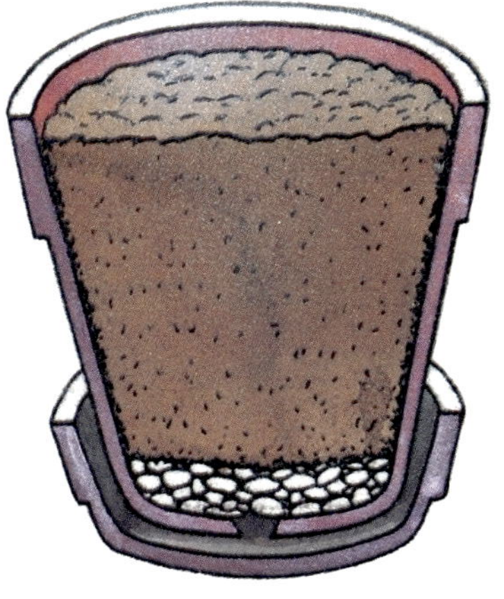

Drainage in Container Gardening

To grow plants successfully in containers, good drainage is essential. Drainage holes need to be covered to keep soil in place: Pieces of broken pottery, fine screening, or a coffee filter are all good choices. You can also add a layer of small stones, perlite, or coarse sand in the bottom of the container. Indoors, or on a porch where dripping water would do damage, place a drip tray under the container to catch excess water.

Gardening in Decorative Containers

When using a decorative container with no drainage holes, place a well-drained pot inside of it in which to actually grow plants. Raise the inner pot on a layer of pebbles to keep it above water level. Peat moss in the space between the inner and outer pots will provide insulation to help stabilize soil temperatures.

The Versatility of Window Boxes

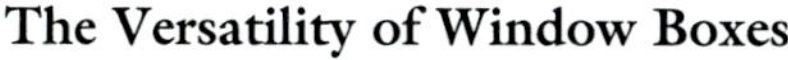

Window boxes are versatile planters that are not just useful on window ledges. They can also hang from porch rails or fences as shown here, perch along the tops of walls, mark the edge of a deck, or line a walk or driveway. Add them wherever you want color without creating a flower bed.

The Many Uses of Hanging Baskets

Hanging baskets provide another almost endless source of color. As shown below, you can hang them from tree limbs; group them at different levels on a porch; or add half-baskets to brighten a blank wall or bare fence.

Zone Map: When's the Last Frost in Your Area?

The United States Department of Agriculture Plant Hardiness Zone Map is a guide designed to link frost dates with regions. It divides the United States into 10 zones based on average minimum winter temperatures, with Zone 1 being the coldest in North America and Zone 10 the warmest. Each zone is further divided into sections that represent 5-degree differences within the 10-degree zone.

This map should only be used as a general guideline, since the lines of separation between zones are not as clear-cut as they appear. Plants recommended for one zone might do well in the southern part of the adjoining colder zone, as well as in the neighboring warmer zone. Factors such as altitude, exposure to wind, and amount of available sunlight also contribute to a plant's winter hardiness. Also note that the indicated temperatures are average minimums—some winters will be colder and others warmer than this figure.

Even though the USDA Plant Hardiness Zone Map is not perfect, it is *the* most useful single guide for determining which plants are likely to survive in your garden and which ones are not.

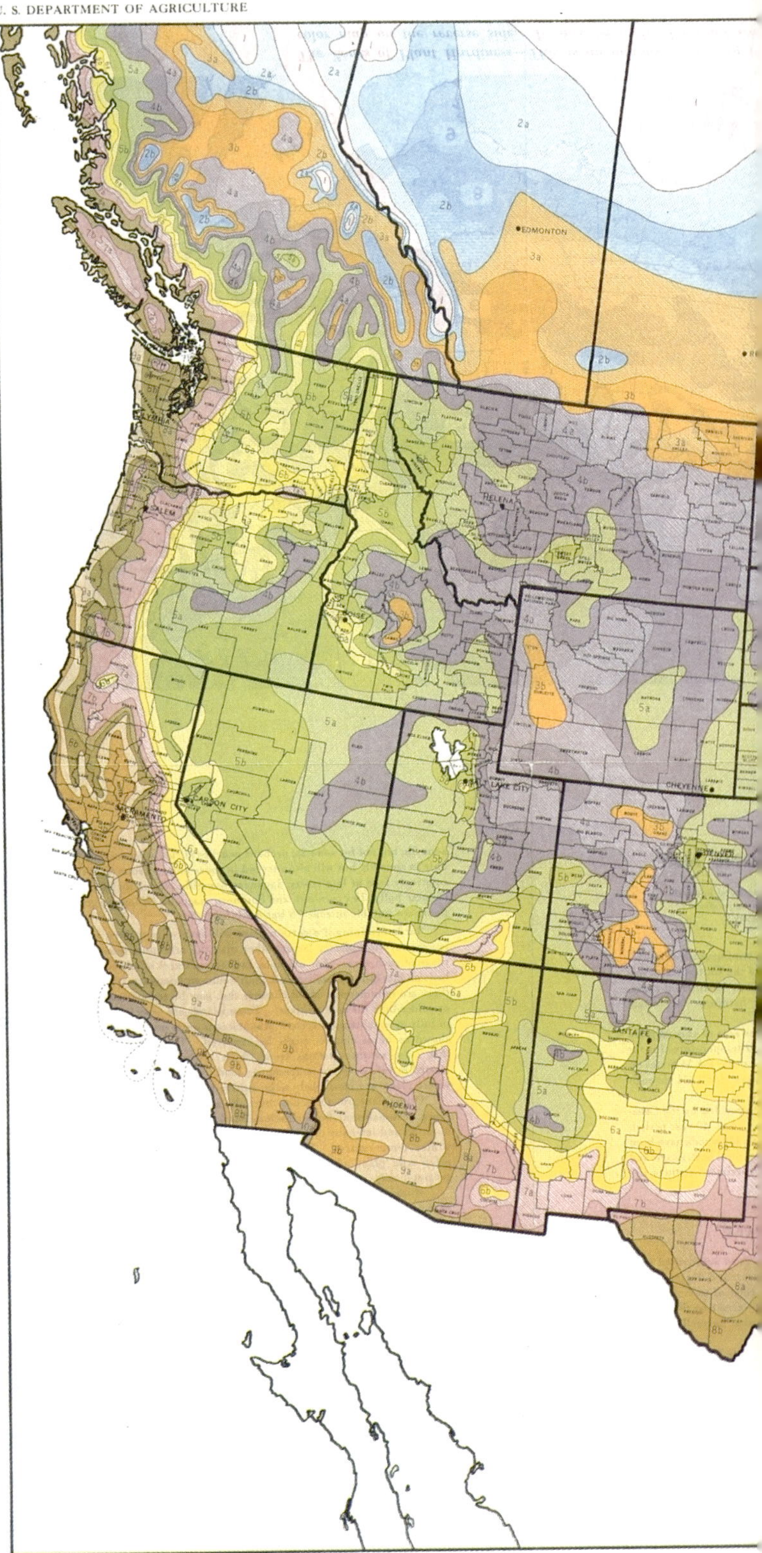

PLANT HARDINESS ZONE MAP

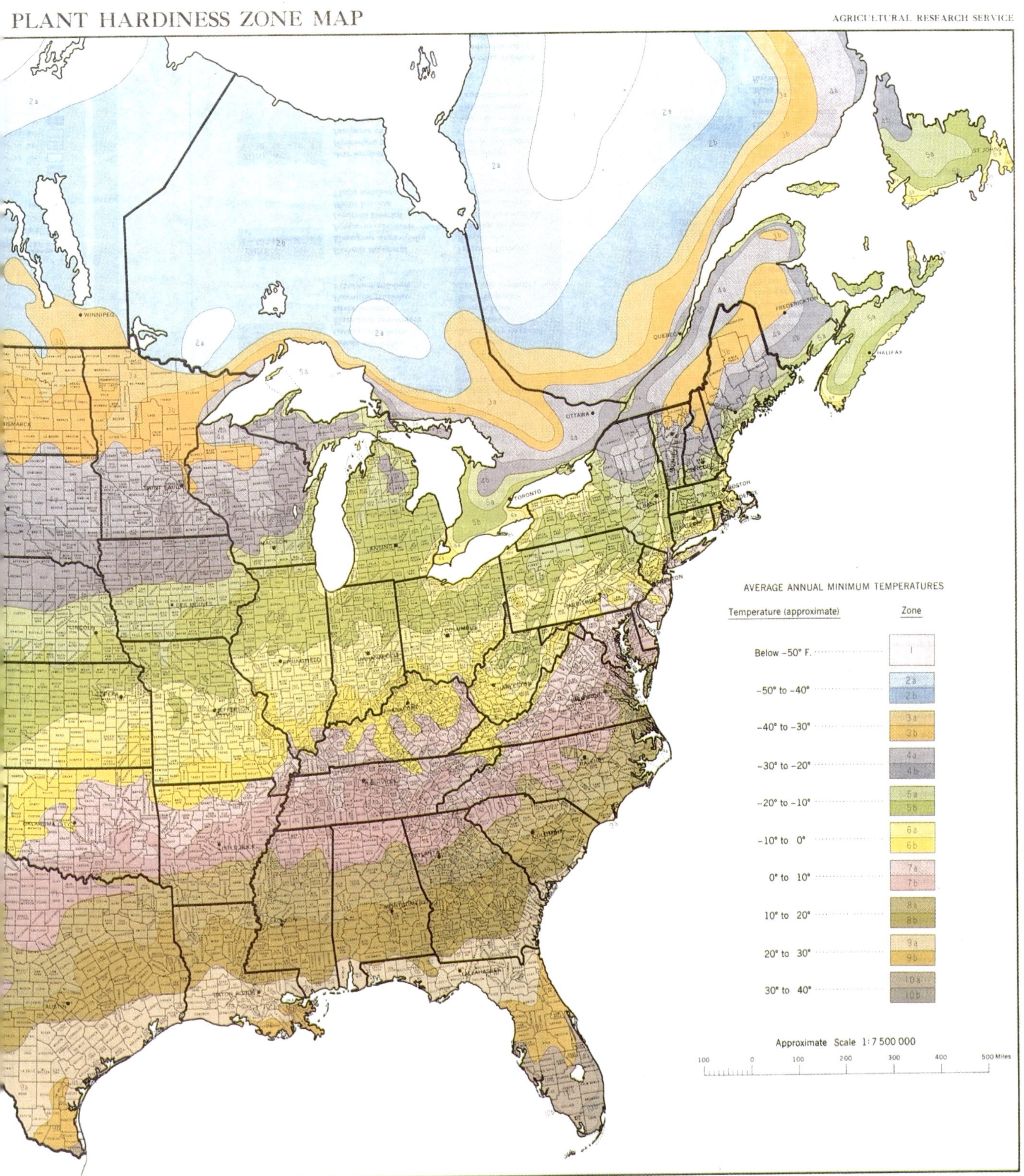

Directory of Annual Delights

This eye-catching garden combines annuals of different colors and sizes.

The plants selected for this directory cover a wide base—some are annuals, others are biennials, still others are perennials in some parts of the world. A few can even be recognized as houseplants. But they can all be used successfully to provide seasonal color outdoors as annuals. Names, descriptions, how-to-grow techniques, propagation, uses, and related species and varieties are all dealt with in depth. Photos are included for each entry.

Whether you live in a suburban home with a large yard or in a condominium 14 stories above the ground with only a windy balcony to plant in, you will find annuals here that will work for you. Given their extensive variety, there are types that can be used to beautify your particular living space, allowing you the opportunity to make entirely different planting choices each year.

Many of the plants listed in the directory are everywhere—a relatively reliable guide to their success rate. Some can be found as started plants at garden centers. Others you will have to start yourself from seed, either from seed packets found on racks locally or from mail order catalogs that offer the greatest selection available. You will be able to familiarize yourself with enough annuals so that you can decide for yourself what will work best for you, depending on your location and the amount of time and effort you want to put into starting and maintaining an annuals garden.

Alyssum, Sweet

Lobularia maritima

Alyssum is covered with thimblelike flowers for months on end, even through the winter in milder climates. A member of the mustard family, alyssum has a pervasive fragrance.

Description: Alyssum grows only a few inches high but spreads as much as 1 foot in diameter. The tiny flowers are closely packed around the small racemes that grow upward as the lower flowers fade. Although white is the most planted color, pink, lavender, and darker shades of violet are also available.

How to grow: Alyssum grows best in full sun in cool weather, but it will tolerate partial shade. Plants will survive light frosts. Space 6 to 8 inches apart. Alyssum will reseed vigorously.

Propagation: By seed. In mildest climates, it can be planted in the fall for cool season display. Otherwise, sow seeds outdoors as soon as the ground can be worked. For earliest bloom, sow seeds indoors 4 to 6 weeks earlier and transplant to the garden while plants are still small. Seeds germinate in 7 to 14 days at 65 to 70° F.

Uses: Alyssum is traditionally used for edging beds and borders. However, it can also tumble over the rocks in a rock garden or be planted in niches between paving stones. Place it where the scent can perfume the air for passersby. It makes a good sunny ground cover for large or small areas. It is good in containers.

Related varieties: 'New Carpet of Snow' is the most planted, but the newer 'Wonderland' series has three distinctive colors: 'White,' 'Rosy-Red,' and 'Deep Purple', the darkest alyssum color so far. Medal-winning 'Rosie O'Day' is a rose color. 'Snow Crystal' is a new, award-winning white variety.

Amaranth, Globe

Gomphrena globosa

Here's a weather- and soil-tolerant plant. This tropical native has small, cloverlike flowers that continue coming through the whole summer season. It's a member of the amaranth family.

Description: Globe amaranth can grow up to 2 feet with newer varieties that are bushy dwarfs. The flowers are about 1 inch in diameter and have a papery texture. The flowers nestle in two large, modified leaves called bracts. The basic color is violet, but varieties have red, orange, pink, and creamy white flowers. The flowers are small, but there are many of them.

How to grow: The only demand for good performance is sun. Plant in the garden after the last frost and, depending on variety, space from 10 to 15 inches apart.

Propagation: By seed. Soak seeds in water for 3 to 4 days before sowing. Sow seeds in place in the garden after last frost. For earlier bloom, start the transplants about 6 to 8 weeks earlier. Seeds germinate in 14 to 21 days at 65 to 75° F.

Uses: The tall varieties are ideal for mid-border. Use dwarf varieties for edging beds, borders, or for a colorful ground cover. Combine them with other plants for container plantings. The tall varieties are especially good for cutting and drying.

Related species: *Gomphrena haageana* has yellow to orange, pinecone-shaped flowers, each about 1 inch in diameter. It also dries well.

Related varieties: 'Buddy' is a compact variety, growing only 9 to 12 inches tall. Flowers are deep purple in color. 'Strawberry Fields' is bright red and grows to 2 feet with long stems. It is splendid for cutting. Several mixtures are offered including white, pink, rose, and reddish-purple flowers.

Aster, China Aster

Callistephus chinensis

From one highly variable species has come a whole range of China asters—singles, semidoubles, and doubles as well as tall, medium, and dwarf—all in a wide range of colors that includes white, pink, yellow, blue, and red.

Description: China asters are available from petite varieties that form compact mounds at 1 foot all the way to tall ones that grow to 2½ feet tall. Bloom times differ, too, with early summer, midsummer, and late summer varieties. For a continuous show, you'll need to pick different varieties and/or stagger sowing dates.

How to grow: China asters grow best in rich soil in full sun. Two disease problems have plagued them in the past: aster yellows, carried by leafhoppers, and fusarium wilt, a soilborne disease. Select disease-resistant varieties when you buy seeds or plants. Spray to control insects. Don't plant them in the same ground two years in a row. Sow seeds indoors 6 to 7 weeks before planting outside. They germinate in 10 to 20 days at 70° F. Otherwise, sow them into the ground outside after the last frost. Each variety blooms only 3 to 4 weeks, so for a continuous show, successive plantings must be two weeks apart.

Propagation: By seed.

Uses: Use China asters in beds and borders. Alternate a space and a plant, then fill the spaces with young plants that bloom later. Tall varieties make superb cut flowers.

Related varieties: 'Pinocchio' is a dwarf strain of mixed colors with a garden mum flower form and garden habit. 'Perfection Mixed' plants grow to 2 feet with 4-inch fully double flowers. 'Super Giants Mixture' grows to 2½ feet with 5-inch double flowers composed of spidery flowers.

Baby's Breath

Gypsophila elegans

Their light, airy texture and petite white or pink flowers make baby's breath a wonderful addition to the garden. This annual is native to the Caucasus and is related to carnations. Because they bloom for only 6 weeks, new seedlings should be started to replace those that have finished blooming.

Description: Annual baby's breath grows to 1½ feet tall, forming an airy bush with many forked branches covered with flowers. Although the flowers, up to ½ inch in diameter, are usually white, there are pink, rose, and carmine forms.

How to grow: Grow in full sun in average, lime-rich garden soil. They grow rapidly and will come into bloom about 8 weeks after germination. Sow new baby's breath every 2 to 4 weeks to assure continuous bloom for the summer.

Propagation: By seed. Sow seeds outdoors in place after the danger of frost has passed. For earlier bloom, sow indoors in peat pots 2 to 3 weeks before planting out, then plant—pot and all. (They grow so rapidly, it is difficult to separate the seedlings, so plant them in a clump.) Germination takes 10 to 15 days at 70° F.

Uses: Baby's breath is effective in borders or cottage gardens. Baby's breath also makes a superb cut flower. It is used primarily as a filler to give unity to arrangements with strong vertical or horizontal lines.

Related species: *Gypsophila paniculata* is a perennial and widely planted. Both single- and double-flowers are found with 'Bristol Fairy,' the most popular species.

Related varieties: The favorite white is 'Covent Garden,' which is also the favorite cut flower strain. 'Kermesina' is a deep rose. 'Red Cloud' has shades ranging from pink to carmine. Mixtures of rose, white, and red are also available.

Bachelor's Button, Cornflower

Centaurea cyanus

The boutonniere flower is reputedly where this favorite got its name. And "cornflower blue" has frequently been used in the fashion trade to merchandise that particular shade. The flowers also come in soft shades of pink, lavender, maroon, red, and white.

Description: Bachelor's buttons grow 1 to 3 feet tall with innumerable round flowers held above the rather sparse, long and narrow, gray-green leaves. The habit of growth is relatively loose.

How to grow: Full sun in average soil is good. For earliest bloom, sow seeds outdoors in the fall so they will start to grow before the first frost and bloom the next spring. They may also be started indoors and transplanted. Otherwise, sow seeds outdoors as early in the spring as the soil can be worked. Thin to 8 to 12 inches apart. Early bloom is heavy and prolific; it tapers off later. Repeat sowings will maintain a lush bloom.

Propagation: By seed. To grow seedlings indoors, germinate at 65° F 4 weeks before planting out. Germination time is 7 to 14 days.

Uses: Bachelor's buttons lend themselves to informal planting, especially with other annuals and perennials in beds and borders. When planting in containers, the gardener should take into consideration their informal growth habit. The flowers dry well, but stems are weak and must be wired for arrangements.

Related species: *C. moschata,* commonly called "sweet sultan," bears sweetly scented, fuzzy, 3- to 4-inch yellow, pink, lavender, or white blossoms. Growing to 2 feet, sweet sultans are good for cutting.

Related varieties: 'Blue Boy' grows to 2½ feet. Award-winning 'Jubilee Gem' is shorter at 12 inches. 'Polka Dot Mixed' and 'Frosty Mixed' have white or pastel contrasts at petal tips.

Begonia, Wax; Fibrous Begonia; Everblooming Begonia

Begonia semperflorens

The brightly colored bedding begonias are equally at home in full sun (except where temperatures stay above 90° F for days on end) or dappled shade and will even bloom moderately well in full but bright shade (where trees are pruned high). From first setting them out until laid low by frost, they'll be packed with white, pink, rose, or red blossoms (some even have white petals edged in red), each flower centered by a cheery yellow eye. Virtually untouched by bugs or blight, their only shortcoming is a relatively narrow color range.

Description: Uniformity is the trademark of most tight mounds of closely packed leaves covered with blossoms. All four flower colors are available with your choice of leaf color: chocolaty-red or shades of green. The deeper or bronze-leaved varieties offer especially eye-catching contrast with flowers. Though not as well known, there are also varieties with double flowers that resemble fat, little rosebuds and others with variegated foliage.

How to grow: Begonias perform well in rich, well-drained soil, but the soil must be allowed to dry between waterings. They'll form tight, compact plants in full sun, with increasingly looser form and fewer flowers as you move them deeper into the shade. Most hybrids will grow 6 to 9 inches high and spread as wide.

Propagation: By seed or cuttings. Most hybrids are grown from seed, but great patience is required. Dustlike seeds (2 million per ounce) must be sown in December or January for large, husky plants by May. Seeds need light to germinate. The seeds should be covered with glass in starting containers to maintain high humidity during germination. Germination temperature is 70 to 85° F and requires 14 to 21 days. Cuttings also root readily. A good way to start plants is on a sunny windowsill during winter.

Uses: Wax begonias lend themselves to large, formal plantings because of their uniform size and shapeliness. They're also suitable in front of summer annual borders and combine well with other cool-colored (blue and green) flowers in mixed plantings and containers. (They tend to be overwhelmed by hot colors.) Even a small planting of begonias in a small pot by a window or door will bloom lustily all summer.
Related varieties: The most popular, dark-leaved kinds are the 'Cocktail' series: 'Brandy,' 'Vodka,' 'Whiskey,' and 'Gin.' Good, green-leaved varieties are found in the 'Olympia' and 'Prelude' series. 'Avalanche' begonias in pink or white are rangier, suited for containers and hanging baskets where their arching growth habit is handsome. 'Charm' begonias, grown only from cuttings, have green foliage marked with white. Calla lily begonias, which can be grown from seed, have green and white variegated foliage and pink flowers. 'Lady Frances' is one of the several double-flowered varieties you'll be able to find at garden centers.

Begonia, Tuberous

Begonia tuberhybrida

A triumph of the breeder's art, tuberous begonias at their biggest have flowers of salad-plate size in fanciful forms and bright colors, even with petal edges tipped in a contrasting color (picotée). These beautiful flowers that grow well in morning sun and light shade have been joined in recent years by new varieties with altogether more modest flowers but many more of them.
Description: The large-flowered tuberous begonias come with many flower types, both upright and pendulous, single or double-flowered, and with frilled or plain petals. Unlike their *semperflorens* cousins, tuberous begonias offer wide color choices: white, pink, rose, red, orange, and yellow. They grow upright with large, arrow-shaped leaves. Both the large- and small-flowered tuberous begonias alternately bear female (lavishly beautiful) and male (single and smaller) flowers. The smaller-flowered tuberous begonias bear many flowers up to 3 inches in diameter.
How to grow: Tuberous begonias grow best in mid-day and afternoon shade; otherwise the foliage will scorch. They need rich, well-drained soil with high organic matter. Allow soil to dry between waterings. The large-flowered varieties easily become top-heavy and require judicious staking, while the smaller-flowered ones can usually support their own growth. Powdery mildew is frequently a problem with tuberous begonias, especially if they are grown where the air around leaves and stems is stagnant. At the first signs of a white powder on leaves, spray with a fungicide.
Propagation: By seed, tubers, or cuttings. Most of the big-flowered tuberous begonias are sold as named-variety tubers. When tiny, pink growth appears on the upper side (with a depression where last year's stem was attached), place the tuber with the hollow side up at soil level in a pot filled with packaged soil mix. Water well once to firm the tuber in the pot and provide a temperature of 65° F. As the top swells and grows, roots will be forming below the surface. Do not allow the soil to dry out, but avoid drenching until the leaves expand. Provide high light until time for planting outside (after all danger of frost has passed, the weather has settled, and the soil has warmed). Carefully plant at the same level as the begonia was growing in the pot.
Uses: Grow the large-flowered kinds as specimen plants in semi-shady locations. Pendulous varieties make good container plants. The new, small-flowered kinds (varieties include 'Memory,' 'Non Stop,' and 'Clips,' all with separate colors) can be used for larger beds, in containers, and in hanging baskets. Watch container plantings carefully to prevent drying out.
Related species: The iron cross begonia *(Begonia masoniana),* a widely grown indoor plant, makes a handsome foliage planting for shade in summer planted directly into the ground or plunged in its own pot. The chartreuse leaves strongly marked with a chocolate-brown iron cross make a bold statement. Be sure to take this plant inside before cool weather starts because it is very frost-sensitive. *Begonia richmondensis* exhibits a graceful, flowing habit; vigorous growth; handsome, glossy leaves; and copious flowers, making it a very popular hanging basket plant in many parts of the country. Flower buds are cherry-red opening to a bright pink. It is easily rooted from cuttings. Morning sun and afternoon shade are ideal. Rex begonias *(Begonia rex)* are foliage plants colored in every conceivable combination: steel-gray, red, pink, green, and with splashes of white. They do well outdoors in the summer in shady spots.

Begonia (continued)

Elatior begonias *(Begonia hiemalis)* are hybrid begonias produced by crossing several species that have created two races of plants providing splendid summer color. One series is upright, good for planters, while the other has a flowing character and is ideal for hanging baskets and other containers to be viewed at eye level or above. Because much of the early development work was done by the Rieger firm in Germany, they are frequently known by this name. Flowers are 1 to 1½ inches in diameter, single, semi-double, and double. Colors are red, orange, pink, and a luscious white that looks green when the light shines through it.
Related varieties: Tubers of large-flowered varieties in separate colors and flower forms are usually available at garden centers and from specialists as named varieties. Smaller, flowered types are available as seed or started plants in garden centers.

Black-Eyed Susan, Gloriosa Daisy

Rudbeckia hirta

This widespread native of the Prairie states has been turned into a horticultural delight. The name "gloriosa daisy" has been applied to the multitude of varieties that have grown out of this prairie weed. Although they're short-lived perennials, they'll bloom the first year and are often grown as annuals.
Description: Varieties of black-eyed Susan grow from 1 to 3 feet tall and are relatively erect. The flowers are available in many warm-toned colors: yellow, gold, orange, russet, and mahogany. Many of them have bands of color intermixed. The single varieties all have a large black or brown center, contrasting with the color surrounding it. Double flowers may reach 6 inches in diameter.
How to grow: Bright sun is the gloriosa daisy's main requirement. It will tolerate poor soil and erratic watering, although it does flourish with better care. Transplant it into the garden in the spring after the last frost. Space plants 10 to 15 inches apart. The taller varieties may need protection from strong winds or staking to keep them from toppling. Cutting the flowers encourages increased blooming.
Propagation: By seed. Treated as biennials or perennials, the seeds can be sown in the garden the preceding summer or fall. For bloom the same season, start seeds indoors 8 to 10 weeks prior to transplanting. Seeds germinate in 5 to 10 days at 70 to 75° F.
Uses: Any sunny location is ideal. Beds, borders, and planting strips will benefit from them. Plant them with ornamental grasses. They'll do well in large containers and are good cut flowers.
Related varieties: 'Goldsturm' has black-centered, single yellow flowers up to 5 inches in diameter. 'Rustic Colors' is composed of many gold, bronze, and mahogany shades. 'Irish Eyes' has golden flowers with green eyes.

Blanket Flower

Gaillardia pulchella

The annual gaillardia is a native of the Plains states to the East Coast. The name "blanket flower" comes from its resemblance to Indian blankets, blooming in yellow, orange, red, and their combinations.
Description: The annual gaillardia grows erect, 1 to 2 feet tall, with narrow leaves 2 inches long and flowers on long stems. In addition to single-flowered varieties, there are doubles with numerous quilled petals. In these, the original orange, red, and yellow colors have been extended to bronze and cream colors.
How to grow: The annual gaillardia will grow well in full sun in any well-drained soil. It does not like clay, excess water, or fertilizer. A fungicide may be needed in areas with high humidity. It continues to perform admirably under dry conditions. Space it from 9 to 15 inches apart.
Propagation: By seed. Barely cover, since gaillardia needs light to germinate. Sow seeds outdoors after the danger of frost has passed. For earlier bloom, sow indoors 4 to 6 weeks prior to planting out. Seeds germinate in 4 to 10 days at 75 to 85° F.
Uses: Plant gaillardia in groups. Grow it in meadows, in the cottage garden, at the edge of lawns, or near woodlands. The flowers are good for cutting.
Related species: Hybrids under the name *G. grandiflora* behave as perennials. Two dwarf forms are 'Goblin' with flowers of deep red, edged in yellow, and 'Yellow Goblin,' a pure yellow. 'Portola Giants,' growing 2½ feet tall, have bronze-colored flowers with yellow tips. The long flower stems are good for cutting.
Related varieties: 'Gaiety' is a mixture of heavily quilled, double flowers in bright yellow, orange, rose, maroon, and bicolors, many tipped with yellow. 'Double Mixed' flowers are 3 inches in diameter in cream, gold, crimson, and bicolors.

China Pink

Dianthus chinensis

These compact plants have a clove scent as well as colorful flowers. They produce blooms in pink, white, rose, scarlet, and crimson; many are bicolored. The original species comes from eastern Asia.

Description: China pinks grow 6 to 12 inches high—clumps of blue-gray foliage surmounted continuously with the single, semi-double, or fringed flowers. In Zones 8 to 10, they will live in the garden for 2 or 3 years as short-lived perennials.

How to grow: Dianthus grows and blooms best during cool temperatures of spring and fall and in cool summer locations. In Zones 9 and 10, they're widely used as winter flowering annuals. Plant them in full sun, in well-drained soil on the alkaline side. (Acid soils can be amended by incorporating lime into the soil before planting.) Plant in the garden after danger of frost has passed. Space 6 to 10 inches apart.

Propagation: By seed. Seeds germinate in 8 to 10 days at 70° F. They may be sown outdoors as soon as the soil is workable. Starting indoors 8 to 10 weeks ahead of planting out will bring an earlier display.

Uses: Use China pinks in rock gardens, in rock walls, or planted in cracks in paving stones. Mass them in at the front of beds or borders. Grow them in containers, alone, or combined with other flowers. They're good cut flowers for small arrangements.

Related species: Sweet William *(Dianthus barbarus)* has a cluster of flowers tops, each flower stalk in pink, white, and red.

Related varieties: The 'Telstar' series has a mixture of scarlet, salmon, rose, pink, and white fringed flowers. Separate colors are available, with 'Telstar Picotée' outstanding. It has crimson flowers edged in white. 'Magic Charms' series is similar, including some speckled flowers. 'Snowfire' has white fringed flowers centered in cherry-red. 'Princess' series is heat-resistant.

Cleome, Spider Flower

Cleome hasslerana

Cleome starts blooming early and flowers continue opening at the top of 6-foot stems. Exceedingly long stamens that extend well beyond the orchidlike flowers—somewhat like a daddy longlegs spider—are what give spider flower its name.

Description: Cleome flowers, with many opening at once, grow in airy racemes 6 to 8 inches in diameter. Flowers are white, pink, or lavender in color. When flowers fade, they are followed by long pods that extend outward from the stem below the terminal raceme. Leaves grow on long stalks from a single stem.

How to grow: Cleome grows well in average soil in full sun or minimal shade. It is very drought-tolerant, although it will look and grow better if it is watered well. Space plants 1 to 3 feet apart.

Propagation: By seed. Sow after the last frost when the ground is warm, later thinning to final spacing. Cleomes may also be started indoors 4 to 6 weeks earlier at a temperature of at least 70° F. Germination time is 10 to 14 days. In the garden, it reseeds prolifically.

Uses: Plant cleome for its height, to back up borders, in the center of island beds, or for statuesque beauty where its dramatic quality stands out. It can also be used as a space-defining hedge, although other plants should hide its bare stems later in the season. Cleome can also be used for tall container plantings. It also makes a good cut flower for use in large bouquets.

Related varieties: 'Helen Campbell' is the most popular white variety. 'Rose Queen' is salmon-pink and 'Ruby Queen' bears rose-colored flowers. Additional color variations including lilac and purple are found in seed mixtures.

Cockscomb, Plumed

Celosia cristata v. plumosa

The name *celosia* comes from the Greek word for "burned." These airy, feather duster look-alikes bear the vibrant colors that aptly fit the name. The exotic plumes make superb dried specimens, retaining their color long after harvest.

Description: Shades ranging from electric reds, yellows, pinks, and oranges to more subtle sand tones are available. Height ranges from 8 to 30 inches. Bloom lasts from June to October.

How to grow: Full sun in average soil is recommended for celosias. Seeds may be sown in the garden after danger of frost has passed and soil has warmed. Initial flowers may last as long as 8 weeks after opening, but removing them will encourage development of side branches and new bloom.

Propagation: By seed. For earlier bloom, celosias may be planted indoors 4 to 5 weeks in advance of planting out. Germination is at 70 to 75° F and takes 10 to 15 days. Plants should not dry out.

Uses: Tall varieties add complementary textures to the center and sides of beds and borders, while the short kinds are good edging plants. They're good container plants, too.

Related species: *Celosia cristata* bears the contorted flowers known as cockscomb. Varieties include: Dwarf 'Jewel Box Mixture' and 'Toreador,' a 20-inch variety with large, red combs.

Related varieties: The tall 2½-foot celosias include 'Forest Fire' with orange-scarlet plumes and 'Golden Triumph,' a golden-yellow. Just shorter is the award-winning 'Century Series' with separate colors of scarlet, red (with bronze foliage), rose, yellow, and cream, as well as a mixture of all colors. Miniatures up to 10 inches are found in the 'Geisha Series' and are especially fluorescent in carmine red, orange, scarlet, and yellow.

Coleus x *hybridus*

Coleus x *hybridus*

Coleus is one of the few plants where late blooming is an asset, for the insignificant flowers detract from the beautiful foliage. Tender perennials, they're very frost-sensitive and are used as annuals except in frost-free areas.

Description: Coleus forms a well-branched, spreading plant up to 2 feet tall and as wide. The leaves vary tremendously, from intricately dissected and lobed forms to broad solids. Colors, too, are varied from solid colors of red, bronze, chartreuse, white, pink, yellow, or green, to variations that combine two or more colors.

How to grow: Coleus is ideal in shade and will excel in northern exposures. It will grow in any well-drained, moist soil. As to light, the deeper the shade, the taller the plant. Leaves are less colorful in deep shade.

Propagation: By seed or by cuttings. Sow seeds 6 to 8 weeks before setting out in warm ground after all danger of frost has passed. Seeds need light to germinate, so do not cover. Seeds germinate in 10 to 15 days at temperatures above 75° F; lower temperatures inhibit germination. Cuttings root quickly and easily—even in water.

Uses: Coleus are unparalleled shade plants. They are useful as ground covers, massed in the front of borders, or grouped in clusters. Coleus grow well in containers. Indoors, they make good foliage plants.

Related varieties: The 'Wizards' have heart-shaped leaves with contrasting colors. 'Rose Wizard' has patches of rose in leaf centers and is edged with green and white to the margins. 'Saber' varieties have narrow, tapered leaves in many colors. The 'Fiji' series features heavily fringed leaves with contrasting color combinations. Small, deeply-lobed leaves distinguish the 'Carefree' series.

Cosmos

Cosmos bipinnatua

Cosmos is one of the fastest-growing annuals. Some varieties reach up to 6 feet by summer's end. They're natives of Mexico.

Description: Cosmos forms a lacy, open plant with flowers 3 to 4 inches in size. These daisies are in pastels of pink, red, white, and lavender with a contrasting yellow center. Foliage is feathery.

How to grow: Cosmos grows best in full sun, but it will bloom acceptably in partial shade. Grow in well-drained soil. It does not need fertilizing. Space at least 12 inches apart. Cosmos needs space and is not easily staked. It reseeds vigorously.

Propagation: By seed. Because it grows so fast, sow outdoors after frost danger has passed. Barely cover seeds, since they need light to germinate. For very early bloom, sow indoors 4 weeks prior to planting out. Germination takes 3 to 7 days at 70 to 75° F.

Uses: Because of its height, cosmos should be planted at the back of borders and grouped against fences or other places as a covering. Its informal habit works best in mixed plantings. Cosmos can also provide height for the center of an island bed. The flowers are good for cutting, especially for informal arrangements.

Related species: *Cosmos sulphureus* is the source of the hot red and yellow colors of cosmos. They're also more compact, growing up to 2 feet in the garden. Bloom is heavy from start until frost. A medal winner, 'Sunny Red,' has 2½-inch, semi-double flowers of vermilion red. Its companion is 'Sunny Gold.'

Related varieties: Most popular is the 'Sensation' series that comes in mixed colors. Separate colors of this series are also available. 'Candy Stripe' has white petals stippled with crimson. 'Sea Shells' has a unique form with rolled, quilled petals. 'Psyche Mixed' bears semi-double flowers.

Dahlia

Dahlia hybrids

From huge, dinner plate-sized blooms down to midget pompoms only 2 inches in diameter, dahlias show as much diversity as any summer flowering plant. Once they start blooming in the summer, there is a continuous flood of flowers until frost. They're tender perennials, forming tuberous roots that may be dug and stored in the fall and replanted the following spring. Where the ground does not freeze, they may be left in the ground over winter.

Description: Dahlias grow from 1 to 5 feet tall. Flowers come in every color except blue and the form is varied: singles; anemone-flowered; peonylike; round, shaggy mops; formal, ball-shaped; and twisted, curled petals. The flowers are carried on long stems above the erect plants. The American Dahlia Society has classified dahlias by both type and size. There are 12 different flower types: single, anemone-flowered, collarette, peony-flowered, formal decorative, informal decorative, ball, pompom, incurved cactus, straight cactus, semi-cactus, and orchid-flowered. Flower size designations are A (large, over 8 inches); B (medium, 6 to 8 inches); BB (4 to 6 inches); M (miniature, not over 4 inches in diameter); Ball (over 3 inches); Miniature Ball (2 to 3½ inches); and Pompom (not over 2 inches in diameter).

How to grow: Dahlias are sun lovers and need air circulation around them. Soil should be fertile, high in organic matter, and moist but well-drained. Incorporate a slow-release fertilizer into the soil before planting. Plant outdoors when the soil is warm and danger of frost has passed. To plant, dig a hole 10 inches deep and as wide. Place the tubers so that the eye is 2 to 3 inches below ground level. Plants growing in pots can be planted at the same level as they were growing in the pot. Space tall varieties 12 to 18 inches apart, reducing the spacing for dwarf plants to as little as 8 inches. Tall varieties, and particularly those with large flowers, must be staked to prevent toppling. Drive the stakes before planting to avoid damaging the plant underground.

Dahlia pinnata 'Racquecourt'

Dahlia 'Modern Trend'

Propagation: By seed, division, or cuttings. Most of the large-flowered varieties are grown from tuberous roots available at garden centers or specialist growers. Each fleshy portion must have a piece of old stem with an eye attached in order to grow (unlike potatoes, which can be sliced into pieces so long as there is an eye in the cut piece). At the end of a summer's growing season, a roughly circular mass of tuberous roots will form a clump. These clumps should be stored in a cool but frost-free location until spring. Where the ground does not freeze, tubers can be left to winter in place. In the spring, divide these pieces (an eye attached to a portion of the stem) just before planting. Sow dahlia seeds 4 to 6 weeks prior to planting out at 70° F. Germination will take 5 to 14 days. Cuttings root in 10 to 15 days.

Uses: Taller varieties can be planted as a hedge with shorter flowers growing in front. Groups of three plants can be effective at the back of the border or in the center of large island beds. Compact varieties can be used in the front of beds and borders or planted in containers. For exhibition, disbudding the side buds will result in substantially larger flowers. Dahlias make good cut flowers, especially those with long stems. They may also be floated in a bowl of water.

Related varieties: There are hundreds of varieties; consult your garden center or a specialist grower. A few tuberous, rooted varieties are: 'Los Angeles,' a semi-cactus variety with deep red flowers and petals tipped in white. 'Canby Charm' is an informal decorative type with pink flowers that can reach a diameter of 12 inches. 'Clown' is golden-yellow with streaks of red in the petals. 'Lavender Chiffon' has blooms up to 7 inches across lavender-shaded flowers. Seed-grown varieties will be available as started plants or can be grown from seeds at home. From seeds, tall varieties include 'Cactus Flowered,' growing to 4 feet with many different flower colors and curved petals. 'Large Flowered, Double, Mixed' will grow to 5 feet and bears large, double and semi-double flowers. Compact varieties include: 'Redskin,' growing up to 15 inches with bronze foliage—a remarkable contrast to the many different flower colors. 'Figaro' grows to 12 inches with semi-double and double flowers.

Daisy, African

Arctotis stoechadifolia

In its native South Africa, arctotis bursts into bloom when the spring rains come, although in gardens plants bloom copiously all summer. A tender perennial, it is grown most commonly as an annual. Like many of the plants in the daisy family from South Africa, it's tough enough to live in hot, dry conditions, but a modicum of moisture will bring out stellar blooms. On dull days and at night, arctotis closes its flowers.

Description: The native species has pearly white flowers centered with steel-blue and encircled with a narrow, yellow band. The flowers are held well above the plant, which forms a compact mound. The leaves are handsome grayish-green that combine well with other colors in the garden. Hybrids with flowers up to 4 inches in diameter have brought other colors—yellow, cream, white, purple, orange, and red.

How to grow: Bright sunny days and cool nights are ideal. Arctotis also thrives in mild winter areas with high winter light. The plant needs full sun and will tolerate lots of abuse. With richer soil and moderate moisture, there are larger flowers and lusher foliage. Fertilize only lightly. Where summers are very hot, arctotis may cease flowering but will resume again when cooler weather prevails.

Propagation: By seed primarily, although cuttings of choice kinds will root quickly. Sow indoors 6 to 8 weeks prior to last frost at 65° F. Seeds germinate in 15 to 20 days. Plant 8 to 10 inches apart at the same depth they were growing in the flat or pot. For later flowers, sow outdoors after danger of frost has passed and the soil has warmed somewhat. Thin garden seedlings to 8 to 10 inches apart.

Uses: Plant arctotis in beds or borders where full sun is available. They will tolerate growing in dry rock gardens for early season bloom. They will also bloom indoors in cool sunrooms or greenhouses.

Daisy, Transvaal; Barberton Daisy

Gerbera jamesonii

A native of South Africa, this is spelled out in both of gerbera's common names: Transvaal being a province and Barberton a city there. A perennial, it is too tender to live through winter except in parts of Zones 9 and 10, but it will bloom the first year from seed.

Description: Gerbera forms a nice rosette of notched, glossy leaves from which the flowers grow 12 to 18 inches high, depending on the variety. Flowers are single, semi-double, or double in shades of pink, orange, red, yellow, and white and are up to 4 inches or more in diameter.

How to grow: They grow best in full sun but will tolerate partial shade. They need moist, well-drained soil high in organic matter and high humidity. Use started plants and plant out after last frost and when the ground has warmed. Make sure to plant at ground level. Depending on the variety, space 12 to 15 inches apart.

Propagation: By seed. Be sure to use fresh seeds. Press seeds into the soil but do not cover; they need light to germinate. Sow 14 to 18 weeks before setting out. Seeds will germinate in 10 days at 70 to 75° F.

Uses: Cluster them at the front or side of a bed, or in a border. Mix them with other plants. Individual flowers last a long time on the plant, but when they're done you need to deadhead to keep new flowers coming. Gerberas are good container plants. As cut flowers, they last up to two weeks.

Related varieties: 'Happipot' is a compact variety with a 10- to 15-inch height. The flowers are single red, rose, pink, salmon, orange, yellow, and cream. 'Parade' is a dwarf series with double flowers in many colors. A taller, cut flower type is 'Gigi,' with 18- to 24-inch stems and 4- to 4½-inch flowers. Many of the flowers are crested.

Dusty Miller

Senecio cineraria, Chrysanthemum cinerariaefolium

The term "dusty miller" originated from the effect of shimmering gray foliage rather than as a name for a particular plant. The name has been commonly applied to a variety of similar plants including *Artemisias, Centaureas,* and *Lychnism.*

Description: *Chrysanthemum cinerariaefolium* grows 1 to 2½ feet tall with finely divided leaflets. It has decorative white daisy flowers about 1½ inches in diameter. *Senecio cineraria* is a bushy subshrub that grows up to 2½ feet tall. The ornamental value is in the finely divided, gray foliage.

How to grow: Preference for both plants is full sun and a rather ordinary, well-drained soil, although they will brighten lightly shaded areas, too. Plant in the garden when the soil has warmed and after danger of frost has passed. Space 8 to 10 inches apart. Pinch the tips of plants to induce shapely branching.

Propagation: By seed or by cuttings. Germinate seeds of *Senecio cineraria* at 75 to 80° F and those of *Chrysanthemum cinerariaefolium* at 65 to 75° F. Germination will take 10 to 15 days. Sow seeds 12 to 14 weeks before planting out.

Uses: These are the classic plants to use in urns with bright summer flowers. They are effective in all kinds of planters. However, they also make great ribbons of light in flower beds and borders. They're especially good to use as a bridge between two clashing colors; to intensify cool colors like blue; or to tone down hot colors.

Related varieties: The most commonly available selection of *C. cinerariaefolium* is 'Silver Lace' with very dissected, feathery leaves. It is not as vigorous a grower as *S. cineraria.* Two varieties of the latter are commonly found: 'Diamond' and 'Silver Dust,' with more silvery and finely divided leaves.

Everlastings, Strawflowers

Limonium

The everlasting sand flower grows up to 2 feet tall on stiff stems. The flowers are silvery white with yellow stems. For drying, cutting before the yellow centers appear is critical. Air-dry upside down in the dark.

Helichrysum bracteatum

These double daisy-shaped flowers grow on long stems 18 to 36 inches tall. They come in a wide range of colors: white, yellow, pink, crimson, and bronze. They must have a long season of growth to develop the flowers before fall. Cut for drying before the yellow centers are visible; use wire stems. Air-dry upside down in the dark.

Statice sinuatum

Statice has clusters of small flowers on long stems up to 36 inches in height and bears off-centered flowers in blue, yellow, rose, and white with other shades less available. Cut the flowers when blooms are at least ¾ open. Air-dry them upside down in the dark.

Lunaria annua

Also called "honesty" or "silver dollar plant," the seedpods are used for dried arrangements. The flowers, which bloom on 2- to 3-foot stems, are mauve or white and can be used in fresh arrangements. Cut the stems for drying when the seedpods are beginning to dry, but before the seeds turn yellow. Air-dry upside down in a dark place.

Xeranthemum annuum

These flowers, also commonly known as "immortelles," grow from 18 to 24 inches tall and have single or double flowers. Flowers are white, pink, rose, violet, and purple. For drying, flowers can be cut at different stages. They retain their colors for a long time after drying. Air-dry upside down in the dark.

Floss Flower

Ageratum houstonianum

Originally from Mexico and Central America, these fluffy flowers in blue-lavender, white, and pink are favorites for window boxes and edging in summer gardens. One interesting aspect of *ageratum* is that the eye sees the color of so-called blue varieties differently than film, which registers them as pink.

Description: Ageratum is covered with fuzzy flowers about ½ inch in diameter on compact, mounding plants from 6 to 10 inches high. They will spread about 10 inches by season's end. Ageratum blooms continuously from planting out after all chance of frost has passed (it is very frost-sensitive) until fall.

How to grow: Grow in any well-drained soil in full sun or partial shade. Space 6 to 10 inches apart for solid color. Occasional deadheading will improve their performance. They need ample water, making sure that leaves never wilt.

Propagation: By seed. Start seeds indoors 6 to 8 weeks before planting. Cover seeds very lightly since they need some light to germinate well. Germination time will be 5 to 8 days at 70° F.

Uses: Plant in the front of borders and beds. They also grow well in hanging baskets, window boxes, and other containers. Most of the newer varieties form compact mounds that provide the scarce blue color so seldom found in annuals. Taller, older varieties make good cut flowers.

Related species: Golden ageratum or *Lonas inodora* has the same flower effect in bright yellow.

Related varieties: Several of the popular blue varieties ranging from light tones to deepest violet are 'Adriatic,' 'Blue Danube,' and 'Blue Blazer.' 'Summer Snow' is white and 'Pink Powderpuffs' is as its name describes. 'Wonder' is a tall variety useful for cutting.

Forget-Me-Not

Myosotis sylvatica

A bed of spring bulbs—such as tulips or daffodils—underplanted with forget-me-nots is a sight to behold. Biennials native to cool, moist areas of Europe and northern Asia, they are usually grown as annuals.

Description: Forget-me-nots are small plants seldom reaching more than 12 inches in height and an equal diameter. The tiny flowers are clustered together in racemes at the top of plants.

How to grow: Forget-me-nots relish cool, moist weather with sun or partial shade. In Zones 8, 9, and 10, seeds can be sown in the fall where plants will bloom in the spring. When planting in the spring, plant as soon as the soil can be worked. When plants have finished blooming, replace them with summer annuals. Forget-me-nots will reseed, but seedlings in colder climates will not bloom until late spring or summer.

Propagation: By seed. For early bloom in cold climates, seed indoors in January, planting seedlings outdoors as soon as the soil can be worked. Seeds germinate in 8 to 14 days at 55 to 70° F. Be sure to cover seeds; they need darkness to germinate. When removing plants that have bloomed, shake the ripened seeds onto the ground where you want blooming plants the next spring.

Uses: Plant forget-me-nots in masses for best results. They're suited for rock gardens, as an edging, or in the front of a border plant. Try them in window boxes and patio planters with spring bulbs. Grow forget-me-nots in meadows, along stream banks, or by ponds.

Related varieties: 'Indigo Compacta' is a darker-colored selection that stays smaller than most varieties. 'Blue Ball' is a compact form with bright blue flowers. 'White Ball' is similar in form but has white blooms. 'Victoria Mixed' combines blue, white, rose, and pink-flowered forms.

Fuchsia, Lady's Ear Drops

Fuchsia hybrida

There are hundreds of named varieties of fuchsias, the beautiful plants with pendulous blossoms that bloom heavily from spring to fall. Most of them have been developed from two species. The name "lady's ear drops" is self-evident, but the name *Fuchsia* is more commonly used. It's named to honor a German botanist by the name of Fuchs.

Description: Garden fuchsias are all more or less woody plants, some having a more erect, bushy habit; others have long, trailing stems from which blossoms hang. The flowers themselves are composed of a calyx, a brightly colored cylinder or tube that points downward, which is topped by flaring, petallike lobes called sepals. The calyx can be single or double, and the sepals are either the same color or contrasting. The calyx and sepals may also be wavy and ruffled.

How to grow: Fuchsias bloom more freely when they get some shade. They're at their best in cool coastal or mountain regions with good humidity, but can be grown successfully in most places as long as they are kept moist. Fuchsias are heavy feeders. Apply a slow-release fertilizer at planting or feed biweekly with a water-soluble fertilizer. Most fuchsias are grown as container or hanging basket plants. For large-blooming plants by mid-May, plant 3 to 5 rooted cuttings in a 10- to 12-inch basket. To develop full and shapely plants, pinch out tips as soon as two sets of leaves have formed after each pinch and continue this process until March 1. Fuchsias are not winter-hardy except in Zones 9 and 10, but they can be stored over winter in temperatures above freezing but below 50° F. Water only enough to keep the root ball from drying out. Light is unnecessary. In January, bring into the light, cut back plants by at least 50 percent, and resume normal watering.

Propagation: By seed or by cuttings. Seeds germinate in 21 to 28 days.

Fuchsia (continued)

Uses: Fuchsias are at their best in hanging baskets where the pendulous flowers can be viewed from below. They are most often placed where they can be seen frequently—on decks, porches, or beside walkways. Upright varieties are eye-catching in containers raised on railings or porch steps. Fuchsias are also grown as standards or in tree form with foliage and flowers flaring out from a single stem grown to the desired height.
Related species: *Fuchsia magellanica* is a small-flowered, hardier species.
Related varieties: Selections are so varied that it is best to choose them in bloom at a nursery or garden center. 'Swingtime,' with double, white calyxes and red sepals, is by far the favorite variety. Double 'Indian Maid' has blue-violet calyxes and red sepals. 'Lena' bears double purple and white flowers. 'Jack Shahan' is a single, pink-flowered variety with a trailing form. 'Marinka', with a multitude of small, red, single flowers, has a counterpart, 'Golden Marinka,' with variegated leaves. 'Gartenmeister Bonstedt' is an old upright variety with numerous firecracker-shaped, red flowers.

Gazania, Treasure Flower

Gazania ringens

This South African flower likes hot, dry summers and cool winters. Gardeners treasure it for its daisylike flowers.
Description: Gazanias grow in rosette form with attractive notched leaves. In many varieties, these are gray-green on top and silver beneath. Flowers rise 8 to 12 inches on short stems. They're white, pink, bronze, red, yellow, orange, and white, contrasting with bright yellow centers. Some varieties have contrasting stripes in the ray petals.
How to grow: Gazanias prefer full sun and moderately fertile, but well-drained soil. The only thing they don't like is heavy soil in hot, humid climates. In Zones 9, 10, and sometimes 8, they'll winter over as perennials. In those areas they'll bloom for 8 or 9 months. Elsewhere, plant out as soon as the danger of frost has passed. Space 8 to 15 inches apart.
Propagation: By seed, cuttings, or division. Sow seeds outdoors after final frost or plant them indoors 4 to 6 weeks earlier. Barely cover seeds; they need light to germinate. Seeds germinate in 15 to 20 days at 70° F. Cuttings taken in the summer root quickly. In Zones 9 and 10, division can be accomplished by cutting clumps apart and replanting the pieces.
Uses: Plant gazanias in the front of beds and borders. Use them as a ground cover in sunny, dry areas or in rock gardens. They're good cut flowers. Gazanias can be potted for bloom indoors. They are good in containers and window boxes.
Related varieties: The 'Daybreak' series blooms in 'Yellow,' 'Orange,' and 'Garden Sun,' combining yellow and orange. The 'Daybreak Mixture' includes pink and white colors. 'Chansonette' has many contrasting colors between the centers and tips of petals. 'Ministar' has a separate 'Yellow' and 'Tangerine,' as well as a mix.

Geranium, Ivy-Leaf

Pelargonium peltatum

Ivy-leafed geraniums have an entirely different character than their zonal geranium cousins. Long, trailing stems make them ideal for containers of all kinds. Their flowers are generally less strident and more toned to the pastel range of their hues. Older varieties are somewhat intolerant of long periods of heat and humidity, but newer varieties are more heat-resistant. The common name springs from the shape of the leaves.
Description: Two distinct groups of ivy-leaf geraniums are available to home gardeners. All of them have the cascading form of all ivy geraniums, but a group of single-flowered varieties from Europe are proving more floriferous and heat-tolerant. Semi-double flowered varieties have less bloom, but still make real impact all summer. Many varieties are available—from miniatures with a spread of only 12 inches through vigorous ones that can grow to 5 feet tall.
How to grow: Ivy-leaf geraniums grow best in cool, coastal, or mountain climates with lots of sun. In other locations they may need partial shade. Ivy-leaf geraniums in containers relish full sun if temperatures are not above 85° F for long stretches. Where this occurs, give them northern or eastern exposure where they can be protected from hot mid-day and afternoon sun. Do not let them dry out. Plant ivy-leaf geraniums outside after danger of frost has passed and the soil is warm.
Propagation: By cuttings or by seed (only one variety so far is seed-grown). Take cuttings from stock plants 10 to 12 weeks prior to planting outside. Pinch tips once or twice to encourage branching.
Uses: Ivy-leafed geraniums are excellent container plants. They develop into shapely hanging baskets clothed with foliage and flowers. As window box plants, they excel and are ideal in patio planters. The single-flowered varieties are also good plants to use as sunny ground covers.

Pelargonium peltatum
'Red Mini Cascade'

Related varieties: Among the heavy flowering, single-flowered varieties (European types), the 'Cascade' series is representative. 'Sofie Cascade' is a light pink with darker shading toward petal centers. 'Bright Cascade' is a glowing red. 'Lila Compact Cascade' is lavender. Good semi-doubles include 'Yale,' rich crimson; 'Galilee,' a very vigorous hot pink; 'Salmon Queen,' 'Snow Queen,' and 'Beauty of Eastbourne', cherry red. The seed-grown variety is 'Summer Showers' and includes red, white, pink, lavender, and plum-colored varieties.

Pelargonium or Geranium; Regal, Martha Washington, or Lady Washington

Pelargonium domesticum

Regal pelargoniums like mild weather and sunny days to perform their best. These plants have large, open-faced flowers above light green, pleated leaves. Exceedingly colorful, they include clear colors of pink, red, white, lavender, and burgundy with the flowers of many varieties marked with bright patches of contrasting colors. Where nights do not go above 60° F, they will continue blooming all summer. In warmer areas, they will take a mid-summer hiatus until cooler nights prevail in the fall. Plant in the garden in the spring when the weather has settled.

Variegated Zonal Geranium

A number of varieties of zonal geraniums are grown for their fancy leaves. Culture is the same as for regular zonals. Probably the most colorful are 'Skies of Italy,' 'Mrs. Cox,' and 'Dolly Varden.' The leaves of 'Ben Franklin,' 'Wilhelm Langguth,' and 'Mrs. Parker' are similar in appearance, rounded with distinct margins of white on the edges.

Scented Geranium

A variety of species pelargoniums have distinctly fragrant leaves when the surface is rubbed. Some have distinctly attractive foliage, but in most the bloom is modest. *Pelargonium crispum* has lemon-scented leaves and a wide number of varieties have been selected from it. *P. odoratissimum* is apple-scented; *P. 'Ninon'* is apricot-scented. *P. grossulariodes* is coconut-scented, while *P. nervosum* has the fragrance of lime. *P. fragrans* smells like nutmeg. One of the most popular is *P. tomentosum,* which has a strong peppermint scent. Its foliage is especially attractive, with felted green leaves of a rich green.

Geranium, Zonal

Pelargonium x *hortorum*

Many gardeners consider zonal geraniums the epitome of summer flowers. Named for the dark, horseshoe-shaped color in the leaves of most varieties, these stalwart garden beauties are tender perennials that must be replanted each year except in the most favored climates. Most *pelargonium* species (true geraniums are hardy perennials) come from South Africa, but through hundreds of years of breeding, the parentage of today's varieties is obscured.

Description: Zonal geraniums are upright bushes covered with red, pink, salmon, white, rose, cherry red, and bicolored flowers on long stems held above the plant. Flower clusters (or umbels) contain many individual flowers and give a burst of color. Plants from 4-inch pots transplanted to the garden in spring will reach up to 18 inches high and wide by the end of summer.

How to grow: Zonal geraniums benefit from full sun and moderate-to-rich, well-drained, moist soil. Incorporate a slow-release fertilizer into the soil at planting time. Plant after all danger of frost has passed and the soil is warm. Space them 12 inches apart. The only other care requirement is deadheading spent blooms.

Propagation: By seed or by cuttings. So far, the only readily available semi-double, flowered varieties are grown from cuttings. The cuttings root easily. Make cuttings 8 to 10 weeks prior to planting out for husky plants. Seed-grown varieties should be started 10 to 12 weeks prior to garden planting. Seeds germinate in 7 to 10 days at 70 to 75° F.

Uses: Zonal geraniums are among the best plants for formal beds. They can provide pockets of color in any sunny spot. Group 3 or more together for color impact in flower borders or along walks and pathways. They're classics in containers, all by themselves, or mixed with other kinds of plants. Geraniums are also grown as standards—a single stem is trained to the desired height with a bushy canopy of flowers and leaves. Zonal geraniums will bloom through the winter in sunny windows.

Geranium (continued)

Related varieties: There are many varieties available at garden centers in the spring. A few popular semi-doubles are: 'Tango,' a bright orange-red with dark foliage; 'Forever Yours,' a vigorous red; 'Blues,' cherry blossom pink with unique rose and white markings near the center of petals; 'Schone Helene,' a 2-toned salmon; and 'Snowmass,' pure white. Seed-grown singles are generally found in series of many colors. Widely planted are 'Orbit,' 'Elite,' 'Ringo,' 'Bandit,' and 'Hollywood' varieties.

Hibiscus, Chinese; Hawaiian Hibiscus; Rose of China

Hibiscus rosa-sinensis

Hardy only in frost-free parts of Zones 9 and 10, hibiscus is widely used as an annual elsewhere. It is a member of the mallow family and is found throughout the year in garden centers as a blooming pot plant for indoor enjoyment, but it can be used outdoors as well.

Description: In nature, they're shrubs up to 15 feet tall, but for summering outdoors they will probably reach a maximum of 3 feet tall and wide. The glossy, evergreen foliage is a handsome background for the large—up to 6-inch—flowers. These flaring bells with a distinctive column of yellow stamens in the center are red, yellow, pink, salmon, orange, or white.

How to grow: Hibiscus needs full sun for best bloom production, but it can tolerate partial shade. Soil should be rich, high in organic matter, and be well-moistened. Hibiscus also grows best in high humidity. Primary use in all but frost-free areas is as a container plant. Apply slow-release fertilizer to the soil before planting the container. Hibiscus can be pruned to make it more shapely by pinching out the tips of young growth to induce branching.

Propagation: By cuttings. Semi-hardwood cuttings root quickly in summer under mist.

Uses: Hibiscus is best used in containers. It can be cut back severely in the spring to maintain its size.

Related species: *Hibiscus rosa-sinensis cooperi* has brightly variegated leaves in pink and white; its blooms are red. *Hibiscus schizopelalus* has finely divided, pink blooms. *Hibiscus moscheutos*, or rose mallow, is a perennial with large flowers. 'Disco Belle Mixed,' grown from seed, has large flowers in red, pink, and white.

Related varieties: There are hundreds of named varieties of *Hibiscus rosa-sinensis*.

Hollyhock

Alcea rosea

These tall, stately plants have long been favored by artists when painting scenes of romantic cottage gardens. Hollyhocks have also been a favorite children's plaything—the flowers can be turned into "Southern Belles" complete with long, ruffled skirts.

Description: Most varieties will grow to 6 feet or taller, the stems surrounded by hibiscuslike flowers in every color except blue. Flowers can be single, semi-double, or double, and are waved or fringed. Leaves are large, round, and coarse.

How to grow: Plant in full sun where there's good air movement to avoid rust. Water and feed heavily and spray with a fungicide if rust develops. Staking may be necessary with very tall varieties or if the site is very windy. Plant 12 to 15 inches apart in clumps. Hollyhocks are prolific reseeders, although they will not come true to type this way. To prevent undesirable colors, deadhead the spent flowers.

Propagation: By seed. Most varieties are biennial but, if seeded early enough indoors, can be treated as annuals for the garden. Sow seeds indoors in February or March for flowers the first year. Barely cover seeds (they need light to germinate) and expect germination in 10 to 24 days at 70° F. Plant outdoors after final frost where they'll bloom from July until frost.

Uses: Since hollyhocks are bold in scale, they add height to the rear of a border. They can also be used as a bright clump beside garden paths or at doorsteps.

Related varieties: 'Powderpuff Mixed' provides a wide range of colors with very double flowers. 'Majorette' produces semi-double and laced flowers on 3-foot stems. 'Summer Carnival' with double blooms will flower as an annual if sown early indoors.

Impatiens, Busy Lizzie, Patience

Impatiens wallerana

Impatiens flower in all colors (except true blue and yellow). Their tidy and mounding habit make them ideal low-maintenance plants. Impatiens were stowaways on trading ships from Africa and naturalized in Central and South America.

Description: Breeders have developed compact, self-branching plants whose flowers are borne above the foliage. Flowers are white, pink, rose, orange, scarlet, burgundy, violet, and many variants. Other varieties have star-shaped patterns of white against colored backgrounds. Double varieties are also grown. Foliage is a deep, glossy green or bronze in color. Most varieties grow 12 to 15 inches high in dappled shade. Heavy watering encourages vigorous growth; higher light dwarfs them.

How to grow: Impatiens will grow in average soil. In cool or coastal areas, impatiens will grow and bloom well if their roots are kept well-watered. In deep shade, bloom diminishes.

Propagation: By seed or by cuttings. Sow seeds 10 to 12 weeks before the last frost date. Impatiens need light to germinate; do not cover seeds, but keep moist. Germination takes 10 to 20 days at 75° F. Use a sterile soil mix, because young impatiens seedlings are subject to damping off disease. A fungicide is recommended. Cuttings root in 10 to 14 days.

Uses: Impatiens can be used in beds, borders, planting strips, and containers. Their mounding habit is beautiful in hanging baskets and planters. Impatiens can be grown indoors in bright, filtered light.

Related varieties: There are many varieties: 'Accent,' 'Dazzler,' 'Impulse,' 'Super Elfin,' and 'Tempo,' to mention a few. Vigorous series such as 'Blitz' or 'Showstopper' are ideal for containers. Double varieties include 'Rosette,' 'Duet,' and 'Confection.'

Impatiens, New Guinea

Impatiens species

When a plant hunting expedition went to Southeast Asia, they made significant discoveries. Species impatiens found there are now being developed into varieties quite different from traditional impatiens.

Description: New Guinea impatiens form compact, succulent subshrubs with branches growing 1 to 2 feet tall by summer's end. Leaves are long and narrow, green, bronze, or purple. Flowers, growing up to 2 inches in diameter, are white, pink, lavender, purple, orange, and red.

How to grow: Fertile, moist soil high in organic matter is preferred by New Guinea impatiens. They are more sun-loving than the other impatiens. They will tolerate more sun if their roots are kept moist. Incorporate a slow-release fertilizer into the soil before planting. They should only be planted after the danger of frost has passed and the ground has warmed. Space 9 to 15 inches apart.

Propagation: By seed or by cuttings. Only two varieties of New Guinea impatiens are available from seed so far. Sow 10 to 12 weeks before planting outside. Germinate at 75 to 80° F. Do not cover, since seeds need light to germinate, but mist to keep moist. Cuttings root quickly and easily in 2 to 3 weeks.

Uses: Impatiens should be used in masses of color in beds and borders. Cluster three or more in groups beside garden features. Plant them in containers and in hanging baskets.

Related varieties: 'Tango,' grown from seed, has fluorescent-orange flowers. 'Sunshine' hybrids, grown from cuttings, are a series that include many with variegated foliage and flowers in all colors—white, pink, red, orange, lavender, and purple. They also have bicolors. Look for constellation and meteorological names: 'Cirrus,' 'Gemini,' etc.

Larkspur, Annual Delphinium

Consolida ambigua

Larkspur resembles the delphinium, with its stately spikes of flowers in cool, pastel colors. Formerly lumped with delphiniums, botanists split them off and named them *Consolida,* an old Latin term for "an undetermined plant."

Description: Larkspur grows up to 4 feet tall with delphiniumlike flowers, single or double, evenly spaced around the long stem above lacy, gray-green foliage. Although blue is favored, larkspur also flowers in pink, salmon, rose, lavender, purple, and white.

How to grow: Grow in moist, but well-drained soil in full sun. If exposed to high winds, larkspur may need staking. It performs best in cool weather. In Zones 7 to 10, seeds may be sown early enough in the fall so that young plants would bloom early in the spring. In other zones, seeds can be sown late in the fall so that they would germinate in the spring. Remove spent blossoms to encourage bloom.

Propagation: By seed. Sow in place because larkspur does not transplant well. Sow in the fall or as soon as the ground can be worked in the spring. For summer and fall blooms in cool climates, successively sow 2 to 3 weeks apart until mid-May.

Uses: Groups of delphinium backing informal annuals can give a cottage garden look. Group them at the side or at the back of the flower border or center them in island beds to lend height. They're good cut flowers and may be dried for winter bouquets.

Related species: Many of the true perennial delphiniums may be grown as summer annuals. 'Pacific' hybrids are widely grown and hybrids of *Delphinium belladonna* are also planted. Compact hybrids (2 to 3 feet high) grown from seed are 'Blue Springs' and 'Blue Fountains.'

Related variety: A favorite is the 'Imperial' series that branches freely from the base.

Lisianthus, Prairie Gentian

Eustoma grandiflorum

This native plant of the Midwest to Mexico has come into vogue recently because of widespread breeding efforts. New hybrids have been developed for flowering pot plants, cut flowers, and garden use. The primary color is a bluish-purple, but it also blooms in pink or white.

Description: Prairie gentians grow up to 3 feet tall, are branched, and are surmounted with cup-shaped, poppylike blooms that open wide in full sunlight. Flowers are about 3 inches in diameter. Although most have single flowers, semi-doubles are also available.

How to grow: Prairie gentians can be grown as annuals by starting them early; otherwise, they are biennials, grown by seeding them the summer before, then wintering them over as small plants in cold frames or heated greenhouses. Grow them in full sun in moist soil. Space 8 to 12 inches apart. Pinch out the growing tips to induce branching and more flowers.

Propagation: By seed. Sow seeds 3 months before planting out when danger of frost has passed. Germination takes 10 to 12 days at 75° F. Because they form a taproot that makes transplanting difficult, prairie gentians should be transplanted to individual pots when they reach the 3-leaf stage. Early growth is slow, picking up when weather warms.

Uses: Grow prairie gentian where you want a strong show of color in moist soils. Because the flower form is so attractive, plant them where they can be viewed close up. They grow well in containers. They are superb as cut flowers.

Related varieties: Varieties include the 'Yodel' series with blue, deep blue, mid-blue, lilac, pink, rose, and white flowers. It is also available as a mixture of all colors. The 'Lion' series is semi-double, offered in white, pink, and blue.

Lobelia

Lobelia erinus

Few flowers have the intense blue provided by some varieties of lobelia. They are perennials, but too tender to live over the winter in most parts of the country and are grown as annuals.

Description: These lobelias have small, round leaves and flowers up to ½ inch in diameter. Some varieties are compact and mounding; others are definite trailers. The most prominent flower color is blue, but there are also crimson, pink, and white varieties. The trailing ones will reach 12 to 18 inches by summer's end; the mounding ones grow 6 to 8 inches high.

How to grow: Lobelia grows best in cool areas or where cool nighttime temperatures moderate the weather. They will bloom well in partial shade if their root areas are mulched and kept moist. Space 4 to 6 inches apart in the garden or in containers.

Propagation: By seed. Seeds are tiny and need light to germinate, so they should not be covered. Start plants indoors 10 to 12 weeks before planting outdoors. Seeds germinate in 20 days at 70 to 80° F. Seedling growth is slow and the early stages should be watched carefully to prevent damping off. A fungicide is recommended. Don't try to separate individual seedlings at transplanting; instead, plant clumps of several seedlings.

Uses: Use the mounding forms for edgings, as pockets in rock gardens, between patio stones, or in the front of taller plantings beside walks and pathways. The trailing varieties can cascade over rock walls and are among the best for containers of all kinds.

Related varieties: Mounding forms include: 'Crystal Palace,' deep blue flowers and bronze foliage; 'Cambridge Blue,' sky-blue flowers; 'Mrs. Clibran,' dark blue with white eyes; and 'Rosamund,' cherry-red. Some trailers are: 'Sapphire,' deep blue with white eyes; 'Blue Cascade,' light blue; and 'White Cascade.'

Marigold, French; American Marigold

Tagetes patula, Tagetes erecta

These all-American plants come in such an array of bright colors over a long season that they're a mainstay of gardeners everywhere.

Description: American marigolds can be tall plants, growing up to 36 inches high, although breeding has produced shorter heights. They have large, fully double flowers in yellow, gold, and orange. French marigolds are bushier and more compact with smaller flowers. Their flowers come in many colors and forms. They usually grow no more than 12 inches. Triploids, a cross between French and American marigolds, resemble French marigolds, but have larger flowers.

How to grow: Marigolds grow best in full sun with moist, well-drained soil, although they will tolerate drier conditions. Plant them outdoors as soon as all danger of frost has passed. Space French marigolds 6 to 10 inches apart; Americans 10 to 18 inches apart. They require no deadheading.

Propagation: Seeds may be sown in place. For earlier bloom, start indoors 4 to 6 weeks prior to outdoor planting. Seeds germinate in 5 to 7 days at 65 to 75° F.

Uses: Grow the taller ones to the center or rear of beds and borders, or as planting pockets in full sun. Plant them in containers.

Related species: *Tagetes tenuifolia,* or signet marigolds, bear many small, yellow or orange flowers. 'Lemon Gem' and 'Tangerine Gem' are two examples.

Related varieties: The flat-petaled, double French marigolds include many series: 'Aurora,' 'Sophia,' and 'Early Spice.' Fully double, crested series include 'Boy,' 'Bonanza,' 'Hero,' 'Little Devil,' and 'Janie.' Single-flowered series are 'Disco' and 'España.' American marigold series include: 'Inca,' 'Perfection,' 'Voyager,' and 'Discovery.'

Marigold, Pot; Field Marigold

Calendula officinalis

These beauties bloom in all shades of white, gold, yellow, and orange. Some varieties have flower petals tipped in contrasting colors. They're known as stalwarts of the cool season garden, growing all winter in Zones 8 to 10.

Description: Cultivated calendulas grow 12 to 24 inches tall with rich, green leaves. Plants will spread 12 to 18 inches. Flowers can be single daisies, semi-double, or fully double. Flower size ranges up to 4 inches in newer varieties.

How to grow: Calendulas thrive in poor to medium soil in full sun with moderate moisture. They will survive several degrees of frost and, if properly hardened off, can be planted in the spring as soon as soil is workable. Plant 10 to 15 inches apart. Pick off the spent blooms for continued bloom. For fall bloom, sow seeds in July. In cool damp weather, mildew is occasionally a problem.

Propagation: By seed. For earliest bloom, sow seeds indoors 4 to 6 weeks early at a temperature of 65 to 70° F. Germination takes 10 to 14 days. After transplanting, the seedlings grow in cooler temperatures (50 to 55° F) until planting outside. Seeds can also be sown outdoors when the soil is workable, then thinned to a 10- to 15-inch spacing. For winter bloom in Zones 8 to 10, seeds should be sown in late fall.

Uses: Plant in beds, borders, planting pockets, and containers in full sun. Calendulas also make good long-lasting cut flowers.

Related varieties: The 'Bon Bon Series' has separate shades of yellow and orange, and a mixture that also includes apricot and soft yellow. The 'Fiesta Gitana Series' bears semi-double flowers in yellow, orange, and a mixture with most of the flowers having dark centers. Taller 'Pacific Beauty' have large flowers on strong stems and are good for cutting.

Meadow Foam, Fried Eggs

Limnanthes douglasii

Here's a West Coast native with many of the attributes of flowers from Mediterranean climates. As the weather warms, rain triggers germination and the flowers quickly come into bloom. It's at its best for spring bloom. *Limnanthes* comes for the Greek word for "marsh." "Fried eggs" (sunny-side up) typifies its look of a great yellow center surrounded by white.

Description: Meadow foam grows up to 1 foot tall with many branches, giving it the appearance of a low mound or bush. It has finely divided, green leaves. The flowers are up to 1 inch in diameter. Typically, they are golden-yellow, surrounded by white, but in some forms the petals are all yellow—still others are all white or white with pink veins.

How to grow: Meadow foam prefers full sun and moist, medium-rich soil. In coastal or mountain areas where the summers remain cool, it will continue blooming all summer. In other climates, enjoy it for spring bloom before weather gets torrid. In nearly frost-free areas of Zones 8, 9, and 10, seeds may be sown in the fall and allowed to overwinter for earliest spring bloom. Space plants 4 to 6 inches apart. Plants will reseed for next year.

Propagation: By seed. Sow seeds in fall in mild climates or as soon as ground can be worked elsewhere. For earlier bloom, start seeds indoors 6 to 8 weeks prior to planting out. Seeds germinate in 14 to 21 days at 65 to 70° F.

Uses: Grow it in rock gardens, near pools or ponds, and along walks and pathways. Use it as an edging for beds or in front of borders.

Related varieties: Named varieties of the typical form are not available. Special forms include: *Limnanthes douglasii sulphurea* with all-yellow flowers; *L. d. nivea,* all white; and *L. d. rosea,* with white flowers veined with rose.

Monkey Flower

Mimulus hybridus

The name "monkey flower" comes from the physical appearance of the flowers or from the name *mimulus,* stemming from a root word meaning "mimic." These low-growing flowers are a good way to brighten up the shade.

Description: Mimulus forms neat, compact mounds seldom reaching over 10 inches in height, but spreading wider. The open-faced flowers are frequently painted with contrasting color markings on the background of yellow, pink, red, burgundy, and other warm-hued tones.

How to grow: Mimulus is not frost-tolerant, but prefers cool weather. It will thrive in moist soil, even in boggy conditions with occasional flooding; it will also bloom beautifully in dappled shade. Plant out after all danger of frost has passed, spacing plants 6 inches apart. Work a slow-release fertilizer into the soil at planting for feeding all summer. Where keeping an even soil moisture level is a problem, a mulch is suggested. Deadheading spent flowers occasionally will improve their appearance.

Propagation: By seed. Sow seeds indoors 10 to 12 days prior to planting outdoors. Do not cover the fine seeds. Germination takes 7 to 14 days at 70 to 75° F.

Uses: Mimulus thrives near ponds, pools, and streams. Grow it in shady borders and, because of its small stature, in front of a border or as an edging. Mimulus is also a perfect container plant. It will also bloom indoors under cool conditions (and high indoor light).

Related varieties: 'Calypso' is a mixture of many colors of 2-inch flowers, both solids and marked bicolors. 'Malibu' is another mixture in shades of red, yellow, and orange. 'Viva' is a single variety with yellow flowers marked with bright red.

Nasturtium

Tropaeolum majus

Nearly every kid who's been near a garden has grown a nasturtium. And today's salad-conscious adult has certainly enjoyed the peppery tang of nasturtium leaves and flowers among the greens. A native of Mexico, they're among our garden favorites.

Description: Nasturtiums started out as vigorous, vinelike plants and many of them still are. Breeders have altered them so that some are now bushy, compact plants only 12 inches tall. The leaves are nearly round. Flowers with bright, open faces have long spurs behind them.

How to grow: Don't overdo the care with nasturtiums. They need full sun in a dry, sandy, well-drained soil. They're at their best in regions with cool, dry summers, although they will grow elsewhere, too. Sow seeds outdoors in the ground after the last frost. Depending on variety, space them 8 to 12 inches apart. The vigorous varieties can only be trained upward by tying them to supports; they have no means of attachment. Nasturtiums will reseed vigorously, but will not be the same colors you planted.

Propagation: By seed. Seed germination takes 7 to 12 days at 65° F. Do not cover the seeds; they need light to germinate.

Uses: Dwarf varieties are good for flower borders, beds, edging paths, and walks. Vining varieties can be tied to fences or posts and trailed from window boxes, hanging baskets, or other containers. Nasturtiums are good cut flowers, too.

Related species: *Tropaeolum peregrinum,* or canary creeper, is a vigorous vine with bright yellow flowers.

Related varieties: 'Dwarf Double Jewel,' in separate colors and a mix, has light yellow, gold, orange, rose, crimson, and brownish-red flowers. It grows 1 foot high. 'Double Gleam' grows to 3 feet with similar flower colors. 'Climbing Mixed' will grow to 6 feet.

Nicotiana, Flowering Tobacco

Nicotiana alata grandiflora

Related to the tobacco plants of commerce, flowering tobacco has been bred for its ornamental value. The flowers are in a variety of colors, including an intriguing lime-green. In addition, flowers have a rich, pervasive scent.

Description: A low rosette of large, flat leaves supports the tall, flowering stems covered with star-shaped flowers. Flower colors include white, pink, maroon, lavender, green, red, and yellow. The plants grow up to 3 feet tall.

How to grow: Nicotiana grows best in fertile, humus-rich, moist, well-drained soil in partial shade, or full sun in cooler areas. They are tough plants that will tolerate high temperatures. Before planting out, incorporate a slow-release fertilizer in the soil. Transplant to the garden when all danger of frost has passed, spacing 8 to 12 inches apart.

Propagation: By seed. In areas with a long growing season, seeds may be sown in place, thinning the seedlings to the right spacing. Elsewhere, start the plants indoors 6 to 8 weeks prior to planting out. Seeds germinate in 10 to 20 days at 70° F. Don't cover seeds; they need light to germinate.

Uses: Nicotiana is a plant that can give much-needed height to beds and borders. Group them in clusters for more impact. They're also good for containers.

Related species: *Nicotiana sylvestris* is a very fragrant species with white flowers. It grows up to 4 feet tall.

Related varieties: The most popular series is 'Nicki' hybrids with separate colors of 'Pink,' 'White,' 'Rose,' and 'Pink,' as well as a mixture. 'Limelight' is a lime-green variety. More compact varieties growing up to 18 inches are the 'Domino' series. It includes 'White,' 'Purple,' 'Red,' 'Lime-Green,' and 'Pink with White Eye,' as well as a mixture.

Ornamental or Flowering Kale *(B. o. acephala)*, Ornamental or Flowering Cabbage *(B. o. capitata)*

Brassica oleracea

The fancy-leaved cousins of our familiar vegetables make a bold statement in the cool season garden. In fact, the ornamental forms are edible, too, but the cabbage is bitter, and when the white, pink, red, and purple leaves are cooked, they turn an unappetizing gray. Tolerant of mild frosts, they're colorful all winter in mild climates.

Description: Bold, round plants whose center leaves (not flowers) color up in cool or cold weather, ornamental cabbage and kale grow 18 to 24 inches in diameter and can grow 18 to 24 inches tall.

How to grow: Their primary use is in the fall because of the short period of cool weather in spring after hard freezes cease. Grow in large pots in a soil mix and feed weekly with a water-soluble fertilizer as recommended on the package. Transplant to the garden or display container in September. Before transplanting, remove tatty bottom leaves. Plant into the ground so that the crown of leaves is flush with the soil surface (roots will grow along the buried stem).

Propagation: By seed. Sow 6 weeks in advance of outdoor planting at 65° F. Do not cover the cabbage seeds since light aids germination. Conversely, cover kale seeds with ¼ inch of soil.

Uses: Kale or cabbage are best planted in areas where you can peer into the center—on slopes, doorsteps, decks, and patios. They're also successful in ground beds and in large plantings.

Related varieties: 'Dynasty Series' cabbage in pink, red, or white have semi-waved leaves. Ornamental kale in red or white include 'Chidori Series,' heavily fringed and especially uniform, and the 'Peacock Series,' which is more compact than others.

Pansy

Viola x *wittrockiana*

Pansies are the ultimate in cool season color, blooming until weather turns torrid. They are related to violets.

Description: Pansies grow on sprawling plants that produce flowers continuously as they grow. Flowers range from 2 inches in diameter up to giants of 5 inches or more. Some have clear colors, but many have the unique faces that are so appealing to kids of all ages. The color range is complete.

How to grow: In mild winter areas, plant as soon as the weather cools in late summer. Even areas with short freezes can enjoy winter pansies; once the weather warms, they'll start opening blossoms. Elsewhere, enjoy them for a short season in the spring. Plant in the garden as soon as the ground can be worked. Space 6 to 9 inches apart. If plants become lank and leggy, shear back halfway to force new growth and bloom. Pansies prefer full sun and cool, moist soil. A bit of shade will help them extend the season in hot climates.

Propagation: By seed. Start seeds 6 to 8 weeks prior to planting out. They will germinate in 10 to 15 days at 68° F. Do not cover seeds; they need light to germinate.

Uses: Plant them anywhere you want spots of color. They are suitable for the front of borders and beds, in small groups among other flowers, in cottage garden plantings, and in containers.

Related species: Several varieties of violas, which are derived from *Viola cornuta* and *V. tricolor* include 'King Henry,' deep violet with a yellow eye; 'Helen Mount,' often called 'Johnny Jump Up' for its yellow and violet-faced flower; and 'Prince John,' a clear yellow.

Related varieties: The largest flowers of all are in the 'Super Majestic Giant' series. The 'Majestic Giants' are somewhat smaller. The most widely planted include these series: 'Crown,' 'Crystal Bowl,' 'Imperial,' 'Maxim,' and 'Universal.'

Petunia

Petunia x *hybrida*

Anyone who's been close to a garden is familiar with petunias, a longtime favorite for undiminished color through a long season. Actually tender perennials, they will flower through the winter in nearly frost-free climates. The name "petunia" comes from a South American word for "tobacco," to which they're related along with tomatoes and potatoes. A plant that has long had the eye of breeders, petunias have flowers with charming variations—open bells, crisped, curled, waved, and doubled up into fluffy balls. The enormous color range even includes yellow.

Description: Garden petunias are divided into two types: multifloras and grandifloras. Each has single and double forms, with grandiflora petunias being larger in each case. Recently, the distinction has become blurred as seed companies have introduced larger-flowered multiflora petunias named 'floribundas.' Always more flowerful and weather-tolerant in the garden than their larger cousins, they were never as popular as the bigger-flowered kinds. Now these new hybrid 'floribundas' are capturing the hearts of gardeners everywhere.

How to grow: Well-drained soil in full sun suits petunias best. They grow well in cool temperatures and will stand a few degrees of frost if plants have been well-hardened before planting. Incorporate a slow-release fertilizer into the soil before planting. Space petunias 12 inches apart. To promote more branching and increased bloom, shear plants back halfway in mid-summer. Deadheading is extremely important—as the plants set seed, flowering is greatly reduced.

Propagation: By seed. Start seeds indoors 10 to 12 weeks prior to planting outdoors. Seeds are very fine and can be more evenly sown by mixing thoroughly with a pinch of sugar. Do not cover the seeds since they need light to germinate. Seeds germinate in 10 to 12 days at 70 to 75° F.

Uses: Beds, borders, walkways, paths, containers—all will accommodate an abundance of petunias. Some varieties are especially recommended for containers, since they mound up and billow over the edges. The multifloras (and 'floribundas') are especially recommended for mass plantings because they give the most flowers per plant, nearly undaunted by drenching rains and high winds. The intricate, double varieties are probably best in containers for greatest enjoyment of their complex flowers. Petunias also make good, informal cut flowers.

Related varieties: Grandifloras: 'SuperCascades,' 'Super Magics,' 'Falcons,' 'Ultras,' and 'Flashes.' All of these are series petunias and are available in many colors—some are veined. Multifloras: 'Madness,' 'Carpet,' and 'Celebrity' are three of the newer series with larger flowers and good garden habits.

Phlox, Annual; Texas Pride

Phlox drummondii

These bright-colored plants originally hail from Texas, but breeders have civilized them to be some of the most dependable garden performers. The name *Phlox* comes from the Greek word meaning "flame," identifying its bright colors.

Description: Annual phloxes grow from 6 inches to 1½ feet tall. The flowers are in large clusters of many colors and in many shapes. Colors include pink, red, rose, white, lavender, scarlet, crimson, and yellow.

How to grow: Annual phloxes grow best in well-drained, sandy soil, high in organic matter. They require full sun and must receive continuous moisture during the growing season. Good air movement around the plants will prevent mildew. Plant in the garden as soon as the danger of frost has passed. Space 6 inches apart. Pinch the tips to encourage branching. At mid-summer, shear the plants back halfway to reinvigorate flowering.

Propagation: By seed. Sow plants outdoors where they are to grow after the last frost is due. Thin to the desired spacing. For earlier bloom, start plants indoors 4 to 6 weeks before setting out. Seeds germinate in 15 to 20 days at 55 to 65° F. Transplant in clumps of several plants to get a full color range.

Uses: Grow phlox in beds or at the front of borders. Use them as edgings. Intermix them with other flowers in informal plantings and cottage gardens. Phlox are good container plants and hold well in water when cut.

Related varieties: 'Petticoat Mix' are very small with a mix of all colors. 'Cecily' is a mixture with a high number of bicolors with contrasting eyes. It is also a dwarf variety. 'Tall Finest Mixed' has large flower heads on plants up to 20 inches tall. 'Twinkle' is a mix of ringed, pointed, starlike flowers.

Poppy, California

Escholtzia californica

California hillsides are covered in spring with the golden-orange of California poppies. Gardeners now have a choice of color—white, rose, scarlet, crimson, or salmon.

Description: Perennials in mild winter areas, California poppies have finely cut, blue-green foliage in contrast to silky flower cups on slender, wiry stems 12 to 15 inches tall.

How to grow: The best planting location for California poppies is sandy, slightly alkaline soil in full sun. They tolerate poor and dry soils as well. In all but Zones 8, 9, and 10, treat them as annuals that bloom best during the cool weather. In cool seasons and maritime climates, they will continue blooming all summer if dead flowers are picked off.

Propagation: Tap-rooted California poppies don't transplant well, so they should be sown in place. In mild winter areas, this is best done in the fall, as small plants will winter over for earliest spring bloom. Elsewhere, sow as early in the spring as the ground can be worked. (If you want to start them indoors, transplant before the taproot is established.) Seeds will germinate in 4 to 10 days when the soil temperature is at 60° F. Water well.

Uses: Grow them in rock walls or rock gardens or as part of naturalized meadow plantings. Reseeding will occur and the offspring of hybrids will revert to the golden-orange colors of their ancestors.

Related varieties: 'Aurantica Orange' is the golden-orange color of the original, although the flowers are larger. 'Ballerina' is composed of semi-double and double flowers in yellow, rose, pink, scarlet, and orange. 'Milky White' is a creamy white selection. 'Thai Silk Pink Shades' has flowers with petals enhanced by wavy edges and fluted form.

Portulaca, Moss Rose

Portulaca grandiflora

Portulaca's profusion of sunny flower colors combined with its toughness make it a natural for difficult garden sites. It will do even better under less difficult conditions. It is a native of Brazil.

Description: Moss roses grow nearly prostrate—a mat of fleshy leaves with stems topped by flowers. The flowers of newer varieties can reach 2 inches in diameter and are in a myriad of jewellike colors—lemon-yellow, gold, orange, crimson, pink, lavender, purple, and white. They're enhanced by the bright button of yellow stamens in the center. There are both single and double varieties. The latter is sparked by extra rows of petals.

How to grow: Full sun; light, sandy soil; and good drainage are musts for portulaca, although they respond to adequate moisture with lusher growth and more flowers. Very frost-tender, they should not be planted outdoors until the danger of frost has passed and the ground is warm. Space them 1 to 2 feet apart. The flowers close at night and on cloudy days. Moss rose reseeds vigorously.

Propagation: Sow in place as soon as danger of frost has passed and the soil is warm. For earlier bloom, start indoors 4 to 6 weeks ahead. Seeds germinate in 10 to 15 days at 70 to 80° F.

Uses: Reserve your problem areas for portulaca. They're good container plants that do not languish if you forget to water them one day.

Related species: *Portulaca oleracea* has ornamental varieties with flowers in white, yellow, rose, and red. 'Wildflower' is a mix grown from seed; selections with even larger flowers are grown by cuttings.

Related varieties: 'Sundance' is a mixture of double-flowered varieties. 'Calypso' and 'Sunnyside' are double-flowered varieties.

Primrose

Primula species and hybrids

Primroses are favored in mild winter areas. They're also spectacular additions to other gardens for early spring color during cool weather. The two most popular varieties for gardens are *P.* x *polyantha,* bred from a number of species with long stems topped by multiple flowers, and *P. acaulis,* featuring many single-stemmed flowers clustered in the center of the plant.

Description: Primrose flowers grow from a rosette of long, narrow leaves. *Acaulis* types will grow up to 8 inches high, while *polyanthus* primroses will grow to 1 foot high. The color range is immense—from a sky color to midnight blue, pinks, reds of all hues, yellow, orange, and lavender. Many of them are centered with a contrasting yellow eye; still others have narrow bands of color in the petals.

How to grow: Where climate is favorable, including the maritime West Coast, they can be grown as perennials. Blooms will start in mid-winter through spring with a reprise of color in the fall when weather cools. Elsewhere, they must be grown for spring bloom. Transplant well-hardened plants into the garden as soon as the ground can be worked. Space them 6 to 10 inches apart. Grow them in soil rich in organic matter and keep them moist. In most places, they're happiest with a canopy of high shade.

Propagation: By seed or by division. To break seed dormancy, store in the refrigerator for 3 to 4 weeks before sowing. Sow seeds 8 to 10 weeks before planting in the garden. Seeds germinate in 10 to 20 days at 70° F.

Uses: Primroses can be a highlight of the spring garden in moist, woodland settings and along woodland paths and walkways. Plant them in pockets by streams or ponds. Interplant them with spring bulbs that bloom at the same time. They're also nice with pansies, forget-me-nots, and other spring flowers. In containers, they can be beautifully combined with all of the above and others. An extra bonus is the delightful fragrance many of them have.

Related species: There are between 400 and 500 species and much interest in growing them, including a Primrose Society for aficionados. *Primula malacoides,* the fairy primrose, grows well in California and other mild areas. It is often found as a pot plant in the spring. *P. auricula* is much grown for variety of flowers, both in the garden and for exhibition at flower shows. *P. japonica* is one of the candelabra species with several whorls of flowers growing on tall stems. It is hardy and a perennial.

Related varieties: Some of the favorite *acaulis* types, all in mixtures and separate colors, are: 'Crown,' 'Festive,' and 'Ducat.' The 'Julian' series is a mixture of miniature plants that are hardy and perennial. The favorite *polyanthus* types are the 'Pacific Giant' series.

Salvia, Scarlet Sage

Salvia splendens

Salvias are best known for their spiky color that is dependable in any climate. Adaptable to full sun or partial shade with equal ease, these tender perennials grown as annuals are related to some of the best perennial plants for the garden as well as to sage, which is used for culinary purposes. A native of Brazil, they come in brilliant red, creamy white, rose, and purplish variants.

Description: The native plants are reported to grow up to 8 feet high. In the garden, 3 feet is about as tall as the largest ones grow. There are dwarf variants that grow only 8 to 12 inches. The spikes of flowers are composed of bright bracts with flowers in the center of each. They are either the same color or contrasting.

How to grow: Salvia is a good, dual-purpose plant that will perform dutifully in full sun or partial shade. It needs average soil and continuous moisture to perform its best. Transplant plants to the garden after danger of frost has passed and the soil is warm. Depending on variety, space from 8 to 12 inches apart.

Propagation: Although seeds can be sown directly in the garden, earlier sowing indoors will bring earlier flowering. Be sure to use fresh seeds, since they lose their viability quickly. Sow the seeds 6 to 8 weeks before the final frost. The seeds germinate in 12 to 15 days at 70 to 75° F. Do not cover the seeds; they need light to germinate. After germination, reduce the temperature to 55° F.

Uses: Salvia provides some of the purest reds and scarlets in the garden world and their vertical growth makes them superb accents in the garden. Plant them as spots of color against other colors. They're a classic combination with blue and white for patriotic plantings. Their ability to bloom well in light shade makes them especially useful with pastel colors that tend to fade in the sun. They also make good container plants.

Salvia (continued)

Related species: *Salvia farinacea* is a perennial in milder climates that is now widely used as an annual throughout the country. Its common name is "mealycup sage" for the grayish bloom on its stems and foliage. It grows 18 to 24 inches tall and produces either blue or white flowers. 'Victoria' is the most popular blue; its counterpart is 'Victoria White.' *Salvia patens,* gentian sage, is named for its rich indigo-blue flowers that have a long blooming season.
Related varieties: 'Carabiniere' grows to 12 inches and, in addition to red, has colors of coral-shrimp pink, orange, blue-violet, and creamy white. 'Red Pillar' is taller and somewhat later. The tallest reds are 'America' and 'Bonfire', which will grow up to 2 feet in the garden.

Sanvitalia, Creeping Zinnia

Sanvitalia procumbens

Although not a zinnia, sanvitalia has enough resemblance to it to fit its common name of "creeping zinnia." Bright, golden-yellow flowers bloom nonstop all summer until frost. A native of Mexico, it is a member of the daisy family.
Description: The plant is a creeper, growing up to 12 inches in diameter with flowers above topping out at 6 inches. The flowers aren't large, but they're so abundant that they nearly obscure the foliage. The purple or brown centers are a pleasing foil to the yellow petals. Most sanvitalias are singles.
How to grow: Sanvitalia prefers full sun, but will adapt to partial shade with less flowering. It is tolerant of most garden conditions. Plant outdoors when all danger of frost has passed and the soil is warm. Space plants 4 to 6 inches apart. Do not overwater or fertilize.
Propagation: By seed. Sow seeds in place when ground has warmed. For earlier bloom, start indoors 4 to 6 weeks before outdoor planting. Seeds germinate in 10 to 15 days at 70° F. Do not cover the seeds; they need light to germinate. Because they do not transplant easily, grow sanvitalias in peat pots that can be planted in the garden, pot and all.
Uses: Since sanvitalia is an annual that likes dry conditions, grow it in rock gardens. Use it as an edging for the front of borders or along sidewalks and paths. It will even bloom near the sunny foundations of houses. It will tolerate dappled shade. Sanvitalia trails well from containers.
Related species: *Wedelia trilobata,* native to Florida and South America, is somewhat similar in appearance with its sunny yellow flowers. It makes a good ground cover in full sun where it roots as it grows.
Related variety: 'Mandarin Orange' brings a new color to sanvitalia.

Snapdragon

Antirrhinum majus

Children love snapdragons because they can snap open the flowers. They are also prized because of their columnar stateliness. Snapdragons endure cool weather and are widely planted for winter color in mild winter areas.
Description: Snapdragons uniformly bear a whorl of flowers atop slender stalks. The best known are ones with snappable flowers, but new kinds have open-faced flowers including double forms. Colors include white, yellow, burgundy, red, pink, orange, and bronze.
How to grow: Plant in rich, well-drained soil with high levels of organic matter. Grow in full sun, fertilize monthly, and water moderately. Space tall varieties 12 inches apart, small varieties 6 inches apart. Pinch tips of young plants to encourage branching. Tall varieties may need staking. After first bloom is finished, pinch off flower spikes to induce new growth and repeat flowering. For cool season bloom in Zones 9 and 10, plant in September.
Propagation: By seed. Germination takes an average of 8 days at 70° F soil temperature. Keep seeds moist, but do not cover, since light is required for germination. For early bloom, sow seeds indoors 6 to 8 weeks before setting outdoors after last frost. Snapdragons may also be sown directly in the garden 6 weeks prior to the last frost when soil is friable.
Uses: Use the tall varieties for the back of the floral border and for cut flowers. Short varieties are good in borders and as edgings for beds. All varieties can be used in containers.
Related varieties: Tall snapdragons include 'Rocket' and open-faced 'Double Madam Butterfly.' Medium varieties, up to 18 inches, are 'Princess' and 'Coronet.' The most popular "mini" is 'Floral Carpet.'

Stock

Matthiola incana

Stock is appreciated for its cool, distinctive colors and exceptional fragrance in cool season gardens. In mild winter regions, it's grown as a winter/early-spring annual for bloom before the weather gets torrid. In maritime or cool mountain climates, it makes a good flower for late spring or summer flowering. A biennial treated as an annual, it's a native of the Mediterranean coast and a member of the mustard family.

Description: Most stock varieties have become well-bred doubles, an upgrade from their wild, single nature. Modern varieties vary in height from 12 to 30 inches, but they're all rather stiff columns surrounded by flowers. The flowers are pink, white, red, rose, purple, and lavender in color.

How to grow: Stock is at its best in the cool, humid weather of foggy, coastal areas, even though some varieties are more heat-tolerant for a longer flowering season elsewhere. Stock will tolerate light frost and is useful for winter bloom in mild climates. Elsewhere, plant as early in the spring as ground can be worked. Moist, well-drained soil high in organic matter is preferred. Stock should be planted in full sun. Space them 8 to 15 inches apart, depending on the size of the variety.

Propagation: By seed. For winter use in mild climates, sow stock in the fall. In other places, sow seeds indoors 6 to 8 weeks prior to when ground can be worked outdoors. Seeds germinate in 7 to 10 days at 70° F. Don't cover the seeds; they need light to germinate. A percentage of seedlings are singles. Doubles are usually the most vigorous seedlings and are lighter in color than the singles.

Uses: Stock is relatively precise in appearance, best suited to formal beds where it can be lined up like soldiers. Plant them where the fragrance reaches passersby—near walks, by doorsteps, and close to heavily frequented places. They're also adaptable to containers, especially if you combine them with informal flowers to break up the rigidity. They're also superb cut flowers, with the scent pervading an entire room.

Matthiola incana annua

Related species: *Matthiola bicornis* has a particularly strong scent at night; the daytime flowers are unexceptional, so plant them discreetly.

Related varieties: 'Trysomic Seven Week' stock is the earliest bloomer. It is more tolerant of heat, offering a complete range of stock colors. It grows 15 inches high. 'Dwarf Stockpot' has separate colors of 'Red,' 'Purple,' 'Rose,' 'White,' or all together in a mix. It grows 8 to 10 inches tall.

Sunflower

Helianthus annuus

Whether giants of the garden at 15 feet tall or barely topping 1 foot, these natives of North America come in a variety of colors and forms. *Helios* is the Greek word for "sun."

Description: Typically growing from 10 to 15 feet tall, sunflowers have coarse leaves and flower heads up to 1 foot or more in diameter. Although they started out as yellow flowers with brown or purple centers, there are now variations with magenta, white, and orange flowers and still others that are fluffy doubles.

How to grow: Sunflowers prefer full sun and will grow in any soil, except one that is light and well-drained. They're very tolerant of heat and drought. The tall varieties may need staking to prevent the wind from toppling them. Plant the tall varieties 12 to 18 inches apart; the dwarf ones, at 9- to 12-inch spacing.

Propagation: By seed. Sow seeds outdoors after final frost. However, for earlier bloom, start indoors 4 to 8 weeks ahead. Seeds germinate in 10 to 20 days at 70 to 85° F.

Uses: The dwarf kinds can be used in beds and borders, while the taller varieties are best at the back of the border. They can be used as a screen or as a clump at the ends of driveways or along fences. The smaller-flowered varieties can also be used as cut flowers.

Related species: *Helianthus debilis* grows 4 to 5 feet tall with yellow or creamy white flowers. *H. giganteus* is the monster sunflower, growing up to 15 feet tall with dinner plate-sized flowers, 12 to 15 inches across.

Related varieties: 'Piccolo' grows to 4 feet and bears rather graceful, 4-inch, semi-double, gold flowers centered in black. 'Sunspot' has 8- to 12-inch blooms on plants only 18 to 24 inches high. 'Large Flowered Mixed' has yellow, red, bronze, and orange flowers on 5-foot plants.

Verbena

Verbena x *hybrida*

Verbenas are garden treasures in areas where few other plants would grow. Some varieties trail; others form mounds of color. Parentage is from species found in subtropical and tropical South America.

Description: The trailing varieties may reach 18 inches in diameter, while the mounding types will grow to about 1 foot high and wide. The flowers are in clusters. The leaves are long, narrow, and notched.

How to grow: Verbenas prefer well-drained, sandy soil with good fertility. They will not grow well in shade or with wet feet. They also need air movement around their leaves to prevent mildew. Plant after all danger of frost has passed. Space plants 12 (upright types) to 18 (trailing types) inches apart.

Propagation: By seed or by cuttings. Verbenas are slow in the early stages. Sow seeds 12 to 14 weeks prior to planting in the garden. Chill the seeds in the refrigerator for 7 days before sowing. Cover the seeds; they need darkness to germinate. They are also sensitive to dampness. Wet the seed flat 24 hours before sowing, sow the seeds without watering, and cover with black plastic until germination. Germination takes 3 to 4 weeks at 75 to 80° F.

Uses: The trailing types are ideal for rock gardens, trailing over walls, and as edgings for garden beds and borders. Use mounding types in beds and borders. Verbena also trails nicely from containers.

Related varieties: 'Showtime' and 'Springtime' series are available as separate colors and as mixes. 'Blaze' is a red variety; 'Crystal,' a white; and 'Delight,' a salmon-pink. These are all trailers. Mounding verbenas include the 'Romance' and 'Sandy' series and 'Trinidad'—a fluorescent rose color. There are also selections grown from cuttings.

Vinca, Madagascar Periwinkle

Catharanthus roseus

These tropical plants, native to Madagascar, stand up well to heat and humidity. Research is now developing new varieties with additional colors beyond the familiar white, pink, and rose of the past.

Description: Flowers are round, 1 to 2 inches in diameter, borne at the tips of branches or shoots, and bear glossy, green leaves. The flowers of many varieties also have a contrasting eye in the center of the bloom. Two forms are grown: somewhat erect types that form moundlike bushes and virtually recumbent trailers.

How to grow: Vinca is at its best in hot conditions—full sun, heat, and high humidity. Grow in warm, rich, well-drained soil. Avoid overwatering to prevent soil-borne diseases. Plant bush types 8 to 12 inches apart; trailing types 12 to 15 inches apart. Avoid planting outdoors until soil is warm.

Propagation: By seed. Sow seeds 12 weeks prior to setting out after last frost. Germination takes 14 to 21 days at a temperature above 70° F. Maintain warm temperatures after germination and be careful not to overwater.

Uses: Trailing types make colorful ground covers and are good edging plants. More upright plants can either back up trailers in the border or combine with other plants. Both types are good container plants. Their heat tolerance makes them ideal for challenging locations.

Related varieties: Creeping kinds include the 'Carpets': 'Dawn,' pink with a rose eye; 'Pink'; 'Snow,' pure white; and 'Magic Carpet Mixture' of all three colors. Uprights include the 'Little' series: 'Blanche,' pure white; 'Bright Eye,' white with a red eye; 'Delicata,' white with a pink eye; and 'Pinkie,' a rosy pink. A new color in vinca is 'Pink Panther,' a fluorescent coral color.

Zinnia

Zinnia elegans

Zinnias are among the favorite American garden flowers, loved for their variety of colors that ranges from bold and brassy to muted pastels.

Description: Zinnias are generally grouped into three classes: tall (up to 2½ feet), intermediate (up to 20 inches), and dwarf (up to 12 inches). Leaves and stems are coarse and rough like sandpaper, while the flowers are in almost every color except blue.

How to grow: Zinnias need full sun and rich, fertile soil high in organic matter. They're best in hot, dry climates. Powdery mildew can be a problem in humid locations. Try to avoid watering from above; plant where there is good air movement. Plant them after the final frost when the soil is warm. Space 6 to 12 inches apart, depending on the size of the variety.

Propagation: By seed. Zinnias grow fast and early bloom can be achieved in most climates by sowing seeds directly into the soil. For earlier bloom, sow seeds indoors 4 weeks prior to planting out. Seeds germinate in 5 to 7 days at 70 to 75° F.

Uses: Dwarf and intermediate varieties can be used in beds and borders or in container plantings. Taller varieties should move to the back of the border or the cutting garden. Zinnias make good cut flowers.

Related species: *Zinnia angustifolia* is a ground-covering species with a prostrate form and single, golden flowers.

Related varieties: Tall varieties: 'Zenith,' hybrids in many separate colors and a mix and 'Giant Flowers, Mixed Colors,' with a variety of colors and flower forms. Medium varieties: 'Border Beauty,' hybrids in separate colors and a mix and 'Cut and Come Again,' with double flowers on long stems. Dwarf varieties: 'Peter Pan,' hybrids with large flowers on short stems and 'Thumbelina,' tiny plants with miniature flowers.